Scoop the Poop
Picking your Battles

Meredith Masony

ISBN: 0692802762
ISBN-13: 978-0692802762

DEDICATION

I would like to dedicate this book to my husband Dave Masony, and to my children Matias, Sophia, and Brian Masony. I would like to thank my sister Brittany Murphy, and my best friends Eric DeYoung and Trey Jayne. I couldn't have done this without the help of my in-laws who have helped with my children throughout this process. I would like to express many thanks to my parents and ALL of my family and friends for putting up with me as I chase my dreams and work towards becoming the best poop scooper that I can possibly be. There will be additional hugs this holiday season as I gift you all with this book. Seriously, everyone gets a book; don't ask for something else.

To all of my MOMosas, I love you. This community means the world to me. Being a Mom is the toughest job on the planet, and YOU ARE ENOUGH. This community has taught me that we need to be happy with who we are, and where we are, in our journey. We are strong. We are relentless. We are AMAZING! Thank you so much for the support, I am so glad you are with me on this journey. Keep calm and MOMosa on!

CONTENTS

Acknowledgments   v

Introduction   vii

1   Secret Poop   11

2   Health Poop   16

3   Getting Started Poop   28

4   Mom Poop   39

5   House Poop   62

6   Marriage Poop   73

7   Dream Poop   100

8   Family Poop   114

9   My Poop   127

10   Hater Poop   146

11   What Does All The Poop Mean?   153

ACKNOWLEDGMENTS

I had thought about writing a book for a few years, but I didn't think I could pull it off. I started my blog, <u>That's Inappropriate</u> to begin my journey, and boy what a journey it has been. I am blessed beyond measure. So many women and men have reached out to tell me that I have helped them, but I think I am the lucky one. I have been able to share my trials with so many people and it has taught me many valuable lessons. What I thought was a "Mommy blog" has turned into a dream job as a creative producer on a burgeoning digital television network at <u>Joy Of Mom</u>, and now my first of hopefully many books.

It wasn't easy to write this book. It was a team effort with my husband, The Business Manager, and my friends and family who helped me through the process. I felt sick to my stomach when I gave my manuscript to my best friend and my sister. I thought, "They are going to see right through me. They are going to read things that I haven't even said out loud." To my surprise they loved the book. Once I knew they enjoyed it, I knew I could publish it.

I have to thank my children, who are my daily inspiration. Raising children is the toughest, dirtiest job on the planet. It can be the most rewarding experience one minute, and then the most heart wrenching the next. My children helped create who I am. I would like to my parents, Tom and Christine and my in-laws, Brian and Nilda for encouraging me on my journey. They may have thought I was crazy at times for chasing this dream, but they were supportive nonetheless. I also want to thank my siblings, my best friends, and my Aunt Gracie and Uncle Craig who have been in my cheering section since the first poorly written blog back in 2014. Thank you to my editor Heather Garcia, who has been a trooper, as I am a dyslexic writer who has no sense of grammar and very little formal training. I am blessed to say that I could write thank yous all day long.

I hope you enjoy this book and I hope you know that you are enough. Each day we get up and we give it our best. Some days our best ends up covered in poop. So I hope you will join me on this journey, grab a shovel, and Scoop the Poop!

SCOOP THE POOP

INTRODUCTION

It had been, "One of those days." I was walking from the kitchen to the laundry room getting ready to switch the sixth load of laundry for the day and there it was… a big pile of steamy poop. I stared at the tower of feces and began to weep. I couldn't stop. The tears were falling like the summer rain. I sat on the floor and curled up into a ball to make myself as small as I possibly could, and I cried. It was one of those ugly cries that had been building for quite some time. As I lay there in that tiny meek ball on the hallway floor I began to laugh mid sob. "It is just poop." I told myself. So I mustered up the energy to get up off the floor and I did what needed to be done. I scooped the poop.

Why am I telling this story? Well, for years I have been working towards accomplishing my dream. I have been spending countless hours writing, creating videos, and creating a community of people who are similar to me. People who fight long and hard to live life to the fullest, while being honest about their daily struggles. The one thing that I have learned throughout this entire journey, is that we need to constantly scoop the poop. Poop comes in many shapes and sizes. Poop is never a "One size fits all" situation, and it can shape shift in a matter of seconds. As a Mother I am the designated poop scooper for everyone in my home, that includes the pets, and sometimes, even the neighbor kids.

I decided that I needed to write this book in order to explain the importance of poop scooping towards a successful life. We have to scoop the poop in both our professional and personal life. We have all been involved in several "Poop Storms" in our lives, and they can make us feel like we can't keep going. Sometimes the mountain of poop is so great that we feel the need to quit. I know how hard it can be. I have quit. What I realized was pretty mind blowing, the poop still needed to be scooped, even though I had given up. The poop continued to accumulate. Quitting did not solve the problem. Quitting only created more poop piles. Piles so high that they became suffocating.

How do we determine what the "Poop" is? Is poop always a curse? Does poop have a silver lining? Our poop is not necessarily always unpleasant. Our poop can be something simple like a long list of errands that need to be taken care of on any given day. Our poop can be a life altering decision. Our poop can be actual, physical, steamy poop. This book is about how we approach the poop. How we prioritize the poop, and how we embrace the poop. Yes, we must embrace the poop.

MEREDITH MASONY

1. SECRET POOP

Poop can be very secretive. Sometimes we don't even realize that we have secret poop. It hides in a dark corner of our brain. It sits and waits. It can be very deceptive. Secret poop happens when we are in denial. Secret poop can stay hidden for years. Secret poop can sit in that dark, tiny, corner of our brains while we are living life. While we are doing the daily carpool drop off lines. While we are rushing from soccer practice to the grocery store. While we are claiming to be "living the dream."

The problem for me was that I was not actually living. I was surviving. There are times in our lives when we simply need to survive. When we have very small children, when we are sleep deprived and only have tiny shreds of sanity remaining, survival mode is required.

By the time I was thirty three, I realized that something was missing in my life. I had been a wife for ten years. I had been a Mom for eight years. I started to become depressed. I was working full time. Life was a constant grind and I felt like I was unable to get off the assembly line. The worst part was that I felt guilty for feeling depressed. I loved my family, but

I knew something was missing from my life. I wasn't passionate about my job, and I had a massive void that needed to be filled. After I put the kids to bed, I sat in the bathroom or in my closet and cried. Often. If my husband found me, he asked why I was crying, but I didn't have an answer.

I woke up in the morning in a zombie state. I struggled to get the kids off to school. I talked myself into getting ready for work. I packed lunches, checked backpacks, planned crock pot meals, and wished I was somewhere else. Yes, that's right. I wished I was somewhere other than my kitchen listening to my children fight over the last pack of fruit snacks. I dreamt about a life that was less stressful and more enjoyable. These thoughts made me cry on the way to drop my kids off at school. These thoughts made me feel like I was the worst Mother on the planet. These thoughts made me feel like a terrible person.

Anxiety and depression are paralyzing. I felt awful, but I didn't know why. I wanted to feel better. I wanted to be happy. I wanted to have passion and fire in my soul. I began to think, "What is wrong with me? Why do I feel this way? What am I doing wrong? Everyone else is happy. Everyone else is living a great life. It's me. I am the problem."

Every time I logged onto Facebook and saw families out at the park, or on vacation, or posting a perfect family picture, I winced in secret shame. Why was everyone else happy? Why were all of these people so put together, so on top of things, so amazing? How did they afford to go on vacation every other week?

How did they keep up with work and life and managing to cook every meal from all locally-sourced, organically grown products while milking a goat in their backyard? What the hell was I doing wrong? I rarely ever posted anything on Facebook. My kids were always running around. I rarely had on pants when I was at home. The dinners I prepared were constant Pinterest fails, and I didn't want anyone to know I was struggling. Really, really struggling. I was a mess. My secret poop was piling up like milk cartons and old-newspapers in a hoarder's house. My secret poop was out of control. My secret poop was contaminating every aspect of my life.

On the surface, I was managing to keep it together for the most part. I was able to take care of the kids, get myself to work, do all of my wifely duties. I was surviving. I was alive. However, I was not living.

I remember going for a run in May of 2014. I remember the exact corner of the street I was on when I had a very scary thought. I said to myself, "What if this is it? What if this is all my life is supposed to be? Am I OK with this?" I wanted to un-think it. It made me nervous and uncomfortable to have even had the thought. My life was a great life. My kids were healthy, my husband was loving and faithful, and has a paid-in-full life insurance policy to boot. I didn't have my dream job, but I had a roof over my head and a full belly. Why was I having these thoughts? Why was I such a selfish asshole?

What kind of monster dreams for more when she has all of this? I couldn't un-think the thought. It just hung in the air. It stayed with me. I had finally let the secret poop out of the dark scary corner of my brain and I acknowledged its existence. I was a monster. I was my own problem. I had spent the last 10 years claiming to be a selfless person. I was in fact a very selfish person who was only pretending. I was pretending to be the happy wife and Mother. I was pretending to be someone who had it all together. I was pretending to live.

Now I had a problem. What was I supposed to do to fix it, to tackle the unleashed pile of poop? I sat down and started to think about the things I love to do. I love to tell stories. I love to talk to people. I love to laugh. I wasn't embracing any of that in my version of "living."

This is the part where some readers will think, "This lady is crazy. She is such a selfish asshole. She has everything she needs and yet she wants more." These people are absolutely entitled to their opinions. I *was* being selfish. I *was* thinking of myself. I *hadn't* put myself first in ten years. I let my dreams wither away. I gave every ounce of my being to my husband and my children and I let the secret poop pile up and fill the dark corners of my mind. I put everyone else first because as women, as Mothers, we are told that we must take care of everyone else before we can take care of ourselves. By doing that, I lost myself. I lost my way. I lost my path.

By putting everyone else first I was hurting myself and my family. I was not the best Mom. I was not the best wife. I was not the best me. I was a Mom-bot who was in survival mode, simply going through the motions.

I needed to find my passion. I needed to live my life. I was simply surviving, and surviving wasn't enough anymore. I wanted more. Admitting to myself that I needed something else was incredibly scary. It went against everything I was taught. Why was I revolting? Why couldn't I just let well enough alone? Why did I need more? What was I searching for? Why couldn't I just be happy?

2. HEALTH POOP

I did my best to keep the secret poop a secret. I didn't talk to my husband about my crazy thoughts. I kept the secret poop to myself. I didn't want my husband to find out that I wanted more. I didn't want him to know how selfish I was. I didn't want him to regret marrying me. I didn't want him to know that I was depressed and scared.

While folding laundry one Saturday, my husband sat down next to me.

> ***Business Manager:*** What is wrong? Why do you always look so sad?
>
> ***Me:*** I'm not sad, this is my face. How do you want me to look while I am folding laundry?

I have always suffered from an awful case of "RBF" Resting Bitch Face, but in this moment, I was lying to him. I had been thinking about how I needed something else in my life. I was thinking that I was meant to do more than fold underwear and socks. That thought once again made me sad. Why wasn't my career enough? Why wasn't being a Mom and a wife enough? What was wrong with me?

My husband suggested that I get out of the house, join a gym, find some friends, get a hobby. I laughed and looked at him, and responded "A hobby? I take care of the kids, the house, I work, I cook, I clean, I take care of everyone. *Those* are my hobbies." He fired back, "I need you to figure out what you need."

I knew he was right. I hadn't told him yet about my deep, dark, secret poop, but I obviously wasn't hiding it as well as I thought. "You're right. I need to do something. I will join a gym." I said. My husband told me about a local gym that was just opening up. He told me he would pick up the kids from school so I could try it out a few days a week in the afternoons. So I went to the gym. I decided to keep my secret poop at bay for a while longer.

I started spending every afternoon at the gym. I was running, lifting weights, and trying to figure out what I was missing in my life. I had always been active, but after having my last baby I had stopped running and working out.

Getting back to the gym did wonders for my mental state. I felt less stress. I was meeting people and I felt like I started finding a direction. I was really thinking about writing a blog and sharing some of my stories with other Moms out there. Moms who would be able to relate. Moms who might feel like me. I started to think that maybe I wasn't alone. Maybe I wasn't a monster.

I started talking to my friends and family about becoming a writer. Not to brag, but I did get a perfect score on the writing portion of my state standardized test back in high school. It wouldn't have won me a Pulitzer, but I had always loved writing. It was a way to escape as a teenager, and I found it alluring still. I loved to make people laugh, so I figured telling stories about the train wreck that was my life was a great place to start. As a Mother of three, I always seemed to have a funny story to tell.

Although I was getting back into shape, and starting to explore other outlets for my poop, I felt sick. I was losing weight. I had a hard time eating, and swallowing, and I had the worst heartburn I had ever had in my life. I was nauseated, dizzy, and tired all of the time. I was actually nervous that I was pregnant. I had my tubes tied back in 2010, but thought, "What if it didn't work?" The fear that I might be pregnant led me to the grocery store to buy a pregnancy test, ice cream, and wine. The wine was to celebrate that I wasn't pregnant. The ice cream was to drown my sorrows in if I was. The single blue line gave me the reassurance that I wasn't pregnant, but my symptoms sent me to my doctor. My doctor then sent me to a gastroenterologist.

I walked into the doctor's office with a list of over the counter medication I was taking along with a list of symptoms I had searched on an internet disease finder. I had written everything down so I could remember to tell him all of the things that were potentially wrong with me.

He took one look at me and told me I was the picture of health. "You are thin and healthy. You have heartburn." He said. I explained that I was tired, nauseous, it was painful to swallow, and I couldn't sleep at night because my heartburn was so bad. I told him that there was something wrong with me. I was *sick*. He gave me a prescription for heartburn medication and told me to come back in a month if I wasn't feeling better.

The next month I was back in his office sicker than ever. My hair had now started to fall out due to my inability to eat. I was scared and I needed answers. He once again told me I was the picture of health. I asked him to do a scope on me but he explained that they are very expensive and assured me that I was fine. " I have good health insurance. I want a scope" I insisted. He told me I was being a bit irrational, but he begrudgingly ordered a scope.

I went to the local surgery center the next week for a scope. Let me just say that I totally get why Michael Jackson was hooked on Propofol. It was the best sleep I had in at least eight years. They asked me to count backwards from ten and I was out by nine. It was glorious. When I woke up I was moved into a waiting room where the doctor met me and my husband. He said that they found a lump in my esophagus, but that he wasn't worried. He needed to run a few tests and do another scope. He was in and out of the room in under three minutes. I looked at my husband and we both got up and walked to the car. I wasn't sure what to think. The first thing I thought when I heard "lump" was of course the "C" word, CANCER. No one wants to say it out loud; like if you say it you will be cursed with it. So, we went home and sat on the couch. I sat quiet for a few minutes, and then logically decided that I needed to cut the lawn.

I jumped on my trusty riding mower and put in my ear-buds. I cut "grass" for about three hours. I just drove around basically cutting dirt. Was I being punished for having all of those awful thoughts about my life? Was I being punished for being depressed? Was I being punished for thinking that I needed more in my life?

I began to think about what would happen if I did in fact have the "C" word. Who would my husband marry? He would need to find someone very quickly. He was thirty four years old, bald, and had three kids. He had been out of the dating scene for eleven years at that point. This was not going to be easy. In my opinion he was a top-of-the-line catch, but selling some woman three kids and my husband's affection for catastrophic gas inducing taco Tuesday might be tough.

We would need to start looking right away. When I got off the mower I asked him to sit down so we could talk. I opened my laptop and went to an online dating site.

Me: We need to find you a wife. Honey, you are bald and have three kids. We need to start looking.

> *Business Manager:* You need to calm down and shut up. No one is going to die.

I explained that I needed to make sure he and the kids would be taken care of when I started to walk towards the light. He did not find any of this humorous, which was not my intent, but I had to laugh. Tense emotional situation make me extremely uncomfortable, so I make jokes. This, in fact, was not a joke though, I really wanted to find him a wife.

The following week I went in for the second procedure. Once again I had the most relaxing twenty minute nap. I woke up in recovery to my husband holing my hand. I asked where the doctor was and he said he had left. I asked what the doctor found and my husband said "It's a tumor, but the doctor said not to worry." So I sat up and asked when the doctor was coming back so I could ask him all of the nine million questions I had. My husband said the doctor wasn't coming back but that he would call us later. "He left? I said. "I wasn't even awake yet. Where did he go? Why would he leave me here like this? What a prick!" I got up and I got dressed. What kind of doctor lets the husband tell the wife that she has a tumor? What an Ass-Hat!

So once again we went home and I got on my riding mower. The grass didn't need to be cut, but I got on anyway and rode around for about two hours. My husband stopped me mid-mow and said the doctor was on the phone. I jumped off and got on the phone. We had a quick conversation about the tumor.

Ass-Hat: I don't believe this is cancer, but I don't really deal with this type of "case."

Me: What do you think I should do?

Ass-Hat: You can wait six months, and then do another scope and we can re-evaluate, or you can see an oncologist.

I thought to myself, "Why on earth would I want to keep a tumor in my esophagus that was blocking the opening to my stomach? I am thirty four years old. I have three kids, a balding husband, and way too much shit to do. I need to know if I have cancer so I can find my husband a wife."

Once again I sat that night with my husband and we talked about the tumor and what kind of wife he would like if I were to kick the bucket.

Me: I know you are drawn to blondes, but is that a sticking point?

Business Manager: *Laughing.* I am firm on her being a blonde. A natural blonde.

We then sat there and I cried for about an hour. It was the hardest discussion we had ever had. So I, of course, deflected and continued to discuss his new wife. She would have big boobs, blonde hair, a sweet ass, and, if possible, a background in gymnastics. She would need to be tidy and a good cook, as well as patient with the kids. I soon realized that my replacement was nothing like me, but that was probably for the best. Perhaps the new wife would be able to post fantastic Pinterest wins and make homemade soap from virgin goat tears. That would be nice.

Two weeks later I found myself in an oncologist's office. He had reviewed my file and started talking about the next steps. I assumed that I would have some type of laparoscopic surgery to remove the tumor and go about my business.

It was not that simple. The doctor informed me that he would need to cut me from belly button to sternum. He needed to remove my esophagus so he could take the tumor out because it was wrapped around the base of my esophagus, basically crushing it. He explained all of the things that could go wrong with the surgery. He explained that I could end up needing a feeding tube, colostomy bag, additional surgeries, and potentially radiation and chemo. While he was talking to me, I don't think I actually heard anything he was saying. I remember his lips moving but I don't remember hearing any sounds coming out. The Business Manager placed his hand on my knee and I snapped back into reality. I looked at the BM and started screaming with my eyes, "Oh my God!"

My husband and I tried to figure out the best time to do the surgery since it was the beginning of the school year, and we would need to coordinate care for the kids. My husband asked if we could do the surgery in a few months so we had time to prepare. The doctor said, "You need to do this now. I don't know if you have cancer. The only way I can determine that is by taking out the tumor. You have a four week window to set up the surgery." Seriously, four weeks was not enough time to get my life sorted. My head was reeling. I was not ready to be a slice and dice piece of fillet-o-fish.

We set the surgery date and spent the next month gearing up for the surgery and five-day hospital stay. My family was amazing. I spent most of that time telling my husband that if it was cancer we would be fine and I would find him a suitable replacement wife. He was a good sport. He must have known that thinking about finding him a wife made me feel better. I know it sounds strange, but I thought that if I had to go, I wanted him and the kids to have someone. I needed to know that they would be taken care of. I needed to know that someone was going to read the kids bedtime stories and tuck them into bed each night. I needed to know that my husband wouldn't be lonely. The new wife would need to be on board with hallway gropings and inappropriate sexting. Yes, sexting with eggplant emojis.

The morning of the surgery we walked into the hospital and I was whisked upstairs to the surgical floor. I kindly asked the nurse to administer something for my nerves. I was quietly thinking that if I pulled out the IV and ran, I could head for Mexico and act like this had never happened. Within a minute of whatever the nurse gave me, I was calm and apparently quite talkative. I told the anesthesiologist that I beat my kids with a flip-flop and he was next if he screwed up. I kissed my husband goodbye and to be honest I don't remember going under anesthesia.

When I opened my eyes, I saw my husband standing over me holding my hand. I tried to say something, but I had a tube in my throat. I looked at him with the burning question in my eyes. He said, "You're okay, it's not cancer." I was elated. It was the best news a mother of three could ever receive. I passed back out. I woke up in the worst pain I had ever experienced. My entire body hurt. I had tubes coming out of everything. I wasn't able to tolerate the pain medications; they were causing nausea, and after the surgery I had I was going to be in big trouble if I vomited. My esophagus was basically ground beef and I could ruin all of the surgeon's work if I upchucked. The next five days were tough. I was only able to take liquid Tylenol. I had been sawed in half and was given liquid Tylenol.

After a week in the hospital, I went home to continue my recovery. This tumor, this experience, taught me a lot about myself. I never would have guessed that my major concern when faced with my own mortality was that I needed to find a wife for my husband and a new Mother for my children. I thought I would have been more concerned with what I was going to miss. I realized that if I was sick and was going to die, I wouldn't actually miss anything. I would be gone, but my husband and the kids would need to continue on. Their lives would not be over. The best thing I could do would be to make sure my family was okay when I left. I am happy I didn't have to find a wife for my husband. No. I am thrilled that I didn't have to do that! But, I am grateful for the experience.

We all have health poop. You may not have experienced a cancer scare, but most people have dealt with something in their lives that caused them to worry about their health and what that meant for their futures. I knew I was sick. I needed to make the doctor listened to me. He did not want to hear me, but I made him listen. We should never let someone tell us that we are wrong when in our guts we know we are right. I have undergone three surgeries over the course of the past two years, and there may be more in the future, but I have to scoop that poop. I do not have a choice. I want to raise my children, fight with my husband, and follow my dreams. That requires major scooping.

I had no idea at the time, but having a tumor caused me to figure out what I needed to do with my life. I realized that life is very short. Life is truly fleeting. Life will pass us by if we let it. I took my new lease on life and I decided that I was going to write a blog. I was going to look for all of the people who were out in the world who were just like me. I decided that I wasn't going to feel alone anymore. I was going to tell my stories. I was going to find my voice.

I had spent years ignoring my voice. I worried about everyone else, and I put my voice last. As Moms, we have a tendency to do that. It can be very detrimental to our health and our spirit. It took me ten years to stop stifling my voice and really listen to what I knew in my gut would ultimately be right for me.

As individuals we need to stop and listen. What are our voices saying? Are we doing what we are truly meant to do? If we are not listening, we need to start. Life flies by at a million miles per hour. We do not have to stop chasing dreams because we are wives or Mothers. I had babies, not a lobotomy. I get to have dreams and goals outside of diaper changing and potty-training, and guess what, we all do. It is never too late. This isn't some cliché statement. At thirty four years old, with three small children, a husband, and a full time job, I began to chase my dream. I got out my shovel and started scooping. We all need to get ready to scoop.

3. GETTING STARTED POOP

After spending a few weeks recovering from my surgery, I decided that I was going to put pen to paper, or, more accurately, punch keys on the keyboard. Either way, in October of 2014 I started my blog. My husband was supportive, but not totally thrilled with my choice. He is a rather private person, I on the other will tell anyone, anything. You want to know about my hemorrhoid's? Sure I'll tell you. You want to know about the trauma my vagina endured during all three of my vaginal deliveries? Pull up a chair.

I started writing the blog anonymously to protect my husband and the children. I wrote about life. I wrote about my frustrations. I wrote about getting peed on in the middle of the night by both dogs and children. It was magical. No one was reading my blogs, so I had freedom to write what I wanted. That's not really true. Some family members were reading my blogs.

If we are being really honest, my Dad wasn't thrilled about my blog and my oldest brother hated it. They had no idea why I would say the things I was saying, or why I would want anyone to read it. At first it hurt my feeling to know that they didn't approve. Why couldn't they just be supportive? Why couldn't they understand that I needed this? It took me a while to figure this out. "Family Poop" requires serious scooping ability.

Despite objection, I really got started. I wrote. I wrote about everything. I wrote about my struggles. I wrote about my fears. I wrote about my sex life. I wrote about very personal topics because I needed to speak the truth. I needed to have a conversation with other wives and Mothers out there who could relate to my experiences. I spent months trying to get published on different sites. I thought my husband was going to die when I told him that I had submitted a piece about our sex life for publication and that it was it was accepted. The original article is below.

What Are The Odds?
(Originally Published in <u>Blunt Moms</u>)

I was sitting on the couch the other night staring blankly at the television. To be honest I don't remember the show, I just remember being tired. It was 10:15; no one was asking me a question, the dishes were done, the laundry was folded, and it was pin drop quiet. That was until my husband walked out of the office and asked, "What are the odds tonight?"

If you are married, you know what this means. This was his clever way of asking if we were going to do it. To be honest, "IT" was the last thing on my mind. I wanted to snuggle up in a blanket and dream about being single and childless for the evening. I wanted to do anything but "IT." I looked at my husband and said "Chances are slim to none." His shitty reply, "Oh, sorry I forgot to make an appointment."

This conversation happens at least once a week. It boggles my mind. I am sitting on the couch close to comatose, and all he wants to do is mount me in my stained t-shirt and flannel pajama pants. So with that statement I continue the conversation. "Aren't you tired?" I ask. "Yes, but I'm never too tired to have sex." I just don't get it. How can he not be too tired for sex? Sometimes I wonder if he asks out of habit, but I think the hard truth is that men are just wired that way. They have a constant genetic drive to continue to spread their seed in order to populate the earth. This drive has forced my husband to find creative ways to bed me.

Almost every night we lay in bed and I find *his* hands in *my* pants, as though they were *his* pants. "Can I help you?" I ask. "Yes!", is always his reply. He usually continues with "I have something for you." Just once, I would like him to say that and it be something other than his penis. He has an arsenal of one-liners that would rival the greatest of porn stars. For example, last month I mentioned that I had terrible cramps. I was trying to give him the heads up that I would not be entertaining him that evening. His insightful reply, "Does your mouth have cramps too?" What a gentleman.

A while back I was in the middle of watching *Grey's Anatomy*. He was pawing on me and trying to get me to follow him into the bedroom. I explained that I was watching my favorite show and that I needed to finish the show if he wanted me to finish him. I am a big Dr. Avery fan. If you don't know who he is, you are missing out. He is a sexy caramel colored treat, big beautiful green eyes, and a set of abs that would make your panties spontaneously drop to the ground. My husband left the room so I could finish watching the show, or so I thought. He walked back in, five minutes later with a picture of Dr. Avery's face taped over his and Avery's six pack abs taped onto his keg. "Are you ready now?" He asked. If nothing else the man is very persistent.

A few weeks ago I had a cold. It wasn't a bad cold, but I had a cough that I couldn't get rid of. I was at the grocery store when I got a text from my husband.

Husband: How are you feeling?

Me: Good.

Husband: Are you still coughing?

Me: Yes.

Husband: I have something for that.

Me: Really?

Husband: Yes. I have some My-Dicks-a drill. You're going to take it when you get home.

Apparently my husband is now a medical doctor.

I am pretty sure that there are wives out there just like me: dealing with husbands that supply them with more than adequate doses of "Penis-cillin" and send them text message from the bedroom asking when they are going to come and get it; dealing with men who were given some type of vaccine to ward off exhaustion and give them the ability to want sex twenty four hours a day.

I am not saying that I don't enjoy sex. Sex is wonderful. But at the end of the day after my blood sucking vampire children and my job have drunk the life out of me, I am exhausted. I have no idea how my husband can be so motivated for sex at the end of the evening. My guess is that he survives so well because he has a wife. A wife who cooks, cleans, raises the children and blows him. Perhaps if I had someone to complete those tasks for me I would be more inclined to play "hide the sausage" before bed? So this year I will be asking Santa for a wife. A wife to do all the shit I don't want to do during the day so I can save up my energy for the sex. My husband will no longer need to make an appointment; it will be first come first serve.

I was over the moon! It took eight months, but I had published my first piece of writing. It was so amazing to read the comments and know that more than my own family members had read something I had written. My husband was embarrassed, but he was a good sport. He didn't like that people he worked with were reading about our sex life. I could already see that this was going to be an issue as I continued to work and get published.

Getting started was not easy. I spent tons of time writing, and rewriting, and doubting myself. I worried that I brought my secret poop out into the light and potentially picked the wrong path. My getting started poop was scary. I constantly questioned myself. What if no one likes what I write? What if I am just making a fool out of myself? When I wasn't working, I was picking up kids, going to the grocery store, and finding time to write. I was going non-stop. I was all over the place, but I was so excited to be chasing my dream, even though I wasn't exactly sure what my dream was yet. I knew I loved writing and telling my stories. I knew I felt compelled to share, but I still wasn't sure what it was all supposed to mean. So I kept scooping the poop.

I continued to write about relatable topics. I, of course, use humor to discuss issues that some may deem inappropriate or crass. I spent a few months trying to get my foot in the door over at <u>The Huffington Post</u>. I spent hours trying to find editor email addresses. I spoke to blogging friends and spammed everyone I could think of to try and claw my way into the publication.

Every week I would submit my blogs to the editorial staff in hopes that I would get published. Weeks would go by and I would check my inbox about every fifteen seconds. I would break down and cry. I would complain to my husband.

Me: *Bawling* Why don't they like my stuff? What is wrong with my stuff?

Business Manager: Be patient.

That only made me angry. I wanted to be a writer. I wanted my voice to be heard. I wanted it NOW! I felt like I had waited my entire life to follow this dream, and all I was getting was closed doors. I was chronically frustrated and that infuriated my husband. I'm sure he wanted me to see some success, but he was tired of my constant whining.

So I continued to submit and on June 1st of 2015 I had an email in my inbox. It was an editor from The Huffington Post. They wanted to publish my piece on granny panties! YES! I was going to be on The Huffington Post. I was going to be proclaiming my love for full coverage underpants! This was it. I was going to be famous! Well, I didn't become famous, but I did have a piece of my writing published in a nationally recognize outlet.

5 Reasons I've Rocked 'Granny Panties' Forever

There has recently been a bit of a rumbling over social media about the fact that granny panties are currently "in style." I am very excited to hear this, but I am not new to the granny panty game. I have never been much of a thong supporter. I do not like having a chronic wedgie, nor do I want to pay more for less underwear. My husband has always been saddened by the fact that I enjoy circus tent, white cotton "day of the week" underwear. To him I say, keep rockin' your Dad bod, and I'll keep my fanny safely concealed.

I am titillated to see that my underwear of choice is now deemed fashionable and hip. It just affirms the fact that I make solid undergarment choices, which obviously translates into my supreme wisdom over all other topics. My reasoning for not wearing thongs, however has nothing to do with the fashion forward trends. Here are the top five reasons I choose to wear said granny panties over super sexy thongs.

1. Let It Breathe: My nether-regions need to stay properly ventilated. I do not want a cotton, or better yet, nylon fabric wadded up my Va-jay, stopping the air flow.

2. Comfort Is Priceless: Yeah, that's right. I like to be comfortable while working my ass off

all day. The last thing I need is to be distracted by an atomic wedgie while my four-year-old is trying to light the house on fire with a starter log on my patio.

3. Shape Shifters: After three kids, my hips have expanded and shifted more times than the tectonic plates on the ocean floor of the western hemisphere. A thong could snap under such pressure. That is actually where the phrase, "You'll shoot your eye out with that thing" came from.

4. No Room At The Inn: I already have three kids, one dog, and a husband stuck so far up my ass, that I literally cannot stick even the tiniest of things up there. There is no room for even the slimmest piece of butt floss.

5. Safety First: Wearing granny panties makes me feel like my pelvis is buckled in. They are like the seat belt of underwear. No one drives a car without buckling up. Click it or ticket.

So I dare you to put on a pair of comfy cotton cheek cuddlers and not grin from ear to ear. More is less. The freedom I feel in my tighty-whities is like nothing else. You may mock my panty lines, but you will never crush my wedgie free spirit.

I was on the front page of <u>The Huffington Post</u>. I was over the moon. The phone rang, and it was my dad.

> **Dad:** I see that you are on that internet magazine talking about your underwear. Why did you do that?

> **Me:** *Trying to keep it together.* It's kind of a big deal, it's <u>The Huffington Post</u>.

> **Dad:** Yes, well why on earth would you talk about underwear?

I just wanted to hear good job. I just wanted to be told that all of my hard work was paying off. I just wanted to feel validated. An editor at a publication that has millions of daily readers had published *my* work. Why can't I talk about underwear? Why can't I have an opinion on full coverage undergarments? Once again I was scooping the poop at an alarming rate. My father was raining down shit all over my parade. I sat at my desk and I put on my metaphorical galoshes and I started to shovel the poop. All I wanted to hear from my father were the words, "Good job." Instead I got poop. Poop. Poop. Poop.

I kept living and writing. I started finding more opportunities to be published and found myself on <u>Today.com</u>, <u>Scary Mommy</u>, <u>POPSUGAR</u>, <u>All 4 Women</u>, <u>Babble</u>, and a few other publications. I was not making any money, but I was getting my work published. I had my first viral post in July of 2015. It was crazy. My website crashed and I was getting hundreds of emails. I was overwhelmed. I kept my head down and I continued to grind. I continued to work full time, take care of the kids, the house, the poop, and I wrote. I felt better when I wrote. I needed it.

It was amazing to find my voice. I knew it was in there. I wasn't doing anything amazing, I was just sharing my stories. I was just letting people in and sharing my thoughts. I began to have less and less fear with my writing. I stopped pulling punches when I wrote and I said exactly what I wanted to say. I wasn't embarrassed or ashamed to speak my mind. I was proud to talk about my underwear.

No matter what your "getting started" poop is, actually getting it started is a scary and unnerving process. The first year of my blog was all about figuring it out and keeping my head down. I was a nervous wreck, but I put in tons of time and effort to find my way into various publications. I shoveled and scooped and cried and started the process over and over again. I brought my secret poop out into the light and I let everyone see it. Scooping our "getting started" poop is unbelievably difficult. It can leave us vulnerable and open for attack. It can leave us worried that it was all for nothing. It can leave us wondering if we made the right choice when we decided to listen to our inner voice and start scooping the poop that is blocking our paths.

4. MOM POOP

I am not a parenting expert. Most of the things I write about and record do have to do with my children. I do have over ten years of parenting experience, but I take that with a grain of salt. As a mother of three, daily life can be a war zone. I have often referred to this phase of my life as "The trenches." I have always thought that my parenting would undoubtedly land all three of my kids on a therapist couch. Life comes at us fast and we often have to perform on little to no sleep while balancing the cooking, cleaning, grocery shopping, laundry, car pool pick up, and 900 million other tasks that need to be completed each day by sunset.

As a Mother, wife, employee, maid, cook, laundress, dog walker, and dream chaser, I can attest to the fact that life is never easy. It is constantly eventful, but being a Mom is the best, hardest, most important job on the planet. As Moms we set very high expectations for ourselves, and we run ourselves ragged trying to maintain them.

I had it all figured out before I had kids. I knew exactly what I would do. I was great at giving advice about parenting. I was going to be the best Mom ever. I was going to be at every event, cook fabulous meals, never forget to pack a lunch, and be on time for everything.

If I could go back in time, I would bitch-slap pre-parenting me and set the record straight. This is the hardest job on the face of the earth. I said a lot of things prior to being a Mom. I am ashamed that I said these things, but I didn't know any better. Now, after doing this job for over ten years, I have to giggle when I hear non-parents, or new parents say these things.

Here are ten of the things I said I would never ever do as a parent.

1. Give my kids junk food: I was going to make my own baby food. I was going to be 100% natural. I tried. I really did, but that policy was just too strict for my house. I have found myself in the check-out line at the grocery store with three screaming kids, right next to the Snickers bars and Kit-Kats on a weekly basis, and 50% of the time, I give in. I'm not proud, just being honest.

2. Give in to a crying baby: I am a firm believer in "Crying it out", it is just much easier said than done. I would put my first child down in his crib and sit at the door and cry as he cried. I would wait until my husband left the hallway to run in and check on him. It did get easier to let the others cry it out, but that

was mostly because I was just too damn busy doing other crap to go in and check on them.

3. Be the last one at pickup: I remember always be the last kid to get picked up from school or sports practice. It was so embarrassing. I always thought that my parents "forgot" me. I never really thought about the fact that they were super busy and they got me as soon as they could. I have actually been on my way home and gotten a call that both my husband and I "forgot" to pick up our son. Talk about turning a shade red; I was so embarrassed. We had miss-communicated, and he was the last one to be picked up from daycare. Guess what, he survived, and so did I.

4. Let my kids sleep in my bed: I said over and over again that kids in the bed was a bad idea. I was not going to share my space with the kids. I would get up and walk them back into their beds. NOT A REALITY. At two o'clock in the morning I was not about to drag my tired ass out of bed to put them back in their own bed. I have managed to survive nine years of children in my bed, so I guess it worked out in the end.

5. Let my kids eat school lunch: I always hated school lunch. I ate it almost every day as a kid. When I was older I packed my own lunch. I was going to be the Mom who packed everyone's lunch every day and made sure to pack a napkin with a love note on it.

In reality, I am lucky if they are sent with lunch three days a week, and the love note may or may not be my wadded up snotty tissue from my bathrobe pocket.

6. Bribe my kids to listen to me: I felt that bribes were the lowest form of parenting. Well, I must currently dwell in Hell, because I bribe on a daily basis. "Did you clean your room? No dessert if you don't clean your room, and it's ice cream tonight." I am too tired to read the proper parenting book to get the job done, so I will continue to bribe my ass off to gain ground each day.

7. Yell and Scream like a lunatic: I grew up in a household of screamers. Everyone yelled at everyone for everything. I am not a fan of yelling. I do however lose my "Mommy shit" at least once a day. It is bound to happen with three kids, and I try to keep it at a level that will not cause the cops to darken my doorway.

8. Sweat the small stuff: I was going to be a proactive parent who cared about the big picture. I wanted to always focus on what really mattered. It's amazing how fast the walls close in when stuck in the trenches of parenting. I know this sounds dramatic, but the daily grind wears me down, and the small stuff becomes a mountain before I know it. For example, keeping the house clean. It seems like a small task, but it is daunting. I

finished cleaning my house one day only to find myself face to face with a turd on the couch. After spending two hours cleaning, it was a bit devastating to find a fresh turd on the couch. Shit really does happen.

9. Give in to their demands: I have been known to have a bit of a rough exterior. I believe that people need to work for their things and it is not beneficial to have them given freely. I want to make sure my kids know the value of hard work. At the same time I can't seem to walk out of a store without buying something for each kid almost every time we go out, and it is so hard to say "No" to three repeating parrots who continue to squawk until I whisper scream "Fine, put it in the cart and be quiet."

10. Drive a Mini-Van: I was going to be the cool Mom who held tightly to class and sophistication. Bawahahaahhaha. That lasted about ten minutes. To be honest, I love my mini-van. It is super awesome and it doubles as a super sweet party van on the weekends. Me and six of my closest friends can bar hop all night in that sexy ride.

So in the end, I do a ton of stuff I admittedly said I would never do. I do it to survive. I do it to remain sane. I do it because life happens. Sanity is a choice. I scoop as much poop as I can each day in order to keep some sanity.

My children do their best to throw as much flaming poop at me as humanly possible. I swear there are days when they join forces and plan my departure to the insane asylum.

When parenting small children, sanity is like a mirage. There are days when the dishes, laundry, and the sounds of running screaming children force me over the edge. I had hit a dramatic parenting low on a spring day a little over a year ago.

Spring break was upon our household like the Bubonic Plague. Kids were crawling all over the place and I had fourteen days' worth of maximum security lock up to look forward to. I work from home which has as many benefits as drawbacks. One major drawback being, I can't get my work done when my kids are home. I tried to find camps to send them to, but that ship had sailed.

The week started out with the common daily issues we all face in our households. There was a ton of screaming, crying, fist fighting, food throwing, running, and tattle telling. I was doing my best to keep it together. I was stressed with work, the demands of the three tiny hemorrhoids, and I was getting ready to have my second surgery for the year. I was not in the best state of mind to say the least.

It was day seven of the break. That morning I got a letter in the mail from my home owners' association stating that we had violated our deed restrictions and owed a $100 fine. I was livid. I had been battling with these Napoleonic retirees for months and I was done.

I loaded everyone into the car and drove to the management office to pay my association fees and address my recent violation. I jumped out of the van to discover that the office was closed. My blood began to boil. I automatically texted my husband a list of obscenities that I could not blurt out in front of the kids. I boldly and feverishly texted that I was on the verge of throat punching someone, and then I buckled myself back into my seat.

On the drive home the kids continued to fight over who was going to watch what when we got home. One kid hit another kid with a book in the backseat and I swung around screaming, "If I have to pull this van over you will not be happy!" My idle threat fell on deaf ears as I continued home with the miniature tyrants screaming that they wanted to swim. I tried to text my husband so that he could attempt to calm me down, but he was in a meeting and couldn't respond.

We entered the house and I ran into my office to check my voice-mails. Just as I had dialed a number I heard two of my kids screaming and crying as though they were being mauled by a grizzly bear. I ran from the office to find them fighting over a stuffed penguin.

At that moment I lost my shit. I couldn't take another second of the screaming and fighting. I grabbed the stuffed penguin and said, "If you're going to fight over it, you're going to lose it!" I then proceeded to make the penguin a double amputee by ripping his arms off. I stuffed him in the garbage can and looked back at my kids. They stood there, in silence, mortified that I had maimed the penguin from *Madagascar*. I shoved his mangled body in the trash can and smacked his beaten head with the lid. He had made his way into an early grave. I stood there in shock. I was now a stuffed animal murderer.

The kids took one look at me and were off like a bat out of hell and ran for their rooms. I followed, screaming hysterically about their constant fighting, and continued my rant for about five more minutes. Nothing in my path was safe. I slammed chairs, threw toys, clothing, and shoes. As I walked past a mirror in the living room I caught a glimpse of myself and I stopped. I looked like a crazy lunatic.

I needed to find my shit and put it back together. I went to the bathroom and cried for a few minutes. I then walked back out to the living room and sat all of the kids on the couch. I apologized. I cried. They cried. We all hugged. My son looked at me and quietly asked if he could have his penguin back. I explained his penguin was now in a better place and he said, "No. He is in a trash can." I tried not to laugh, but I did. My oldest chimed in with, "Yeah buddy, it's gone. Mom went crazy on that penguin."

It is most definitely a day that I won't forget. It was one of my worst parenting moments, but it taught me a very specific lesson. I simply can't do it all. I can't take care of three kids, work from home, take care of the house, chase my dream of becoming a writer, and keep any kind of sanity. I called my boss that evening and asked her for a week off so that I could properly do my most vital job, be a Mom.

So the reason I am talking about my worst parenting moment, is to reiterate that it too shall pass. I know that my limits are real and must be acknowledged. We all fail; it's what happens next that matters most. As parents we keep going. We push through the poop and find our way to the other side. Real nitty gritty parenting is rarely perfect or pretty. There will be plenty of Pinterest fails along the way. I'm pretty sure my youngest will never look at a stuffed penguin the same ever again, but I am hopeful he will remember the conversation we had when I apologized for losing my shit. I hope that when he gets married and has a child, he will be able to think back and understand the stress that I felt in that mind numbing moment and know that I never meant to hurt his feelings. I simply lost my shit and needed to "have a moment" that was unattractive yet educational. I had to keep scooping. My parenting life has been spent in the trenches, and the scooping gets fierce down there.

The trenches are a tough place to be. I had no idea what it meant to be tired before having kids. I secretly hate anyone who takes naps. I distinctly remember a very trying weekend a while back. I found myself asking the same questions over and over. I had several arguments about teeth brushing, cleaning up toys, going to bed, and fist fighting. It led me to a question that left me quietly sedated while on the couch watching TV. "What if once were enough?" What would happen if I asked my kids or my husband to do something once, and it actually happened the first time?

Friday morning, while in a mad panic to get my five year old to school on time, I asked my ten year old and and my seven year old to brush their teeth. "We're not getting out of the car so we don't have to brush our teeth," was the reply. "I asked you to brush your teeth, go do it." Five minutes later I found them both on the ground spilling mouth wash in each other's hair. Bubble gum flavored blue mouth wash poured all over the floor. "WHAT ARE YOU DOING?" I screamed. "We're brushing our teeth." Were they freaking serious? This was not what I had asked them to do. "Get off the floor and brush your teeth." I went back in three minutes later and one was on the toilet while the other was coloring. "Get up and brush your teeth or I am going to lose it." My empty threats just hung in the air like a stale fart. Finally they exited the bathroom and I could only hope they brushed their teeth. Most days their breath smells like a cat litter box, but there is only so much I can do.

We got to school and dropped off my five year old. The next stop was the grocery store. I began to speed shop so we could get out of there without any major issues. I was literally running up and down aisles throwing essentials in the cart, hoping to make it out of there without spending two hundred dollars, which never happens. I looked over and see ten year old running his fingers across every item on the shelf. "Don't touch those, they are going to fall." We continued moving. I looked back again and saw him continuing to man-handle the Captain Crunch. "Please do not touch the items on the shelf." I was almost on a full sprint as we passed the goldfish when

I heard a big crash. I looked back and saw a pile of Ritz Bits crackers littering the polished floor. "Hurry up and pick those up!" I whisper-scream at him. Most Moms know what that it. It is when the angry parent crouches down and whispers in a mean scary voice, while smiling, hoping that the wayward child will finally listen to the words coming out of the parent's mouth. The embarrassment swelled up inside me as other customers begin to watch the situation.

We left the store and headed home to start the rest of the day. I was already exhausted and it was only ten o'clock in the morning. The day moved on without too much drama. We had dinner that night and finished our bedtime routine. I began to tell my husband about our day and I started to complain about the excessive number of times I seemed to ask the same question. I explained that I couldn't take another day of begging and pleading over teeth brushing and bed times. He looked at me and said, "Well, if you would punish them when they don't listen maybe they would do it the first time." To say I lost my shit would be an understatement. I am amazed that Google earth didn't get an image of me shoving my husband's head directly up his anus.

If I punished them every time they didn't do something I asked the first time, they would never be off punishment. Dealing with three children under the age of ten is like trying to control an impending volcanic eruption. They are a force of nature that can tear houses into pieces. So after I helped remove my husband's head from his sphincter, I realized that he too suffers from this disorder.

Me: Can you wash the dishes?

Business Manager: Yes, I'll get to it.

Me: *Switches laundry. Cleans up toys.*

Business Manager: Magically moved from the kitchen to the couch.

Me: I thought you were going to do the dishes?

Business Manager: They are soaking.

Me: Really? Why do they have to soak? We had soup.

Me: *Counting in my head so that I don't throw a flip flop at him.*

Me: Are you going to do the dishes?

Business Manager: I will get to it.

One hour of Sports Center later

Me: *Finishes washing the dishes.*

Business Manager: Honey, (sweet voice insertion) I said I would do the dishes.

I smile at him thinking to myself, I thought about doing you tonight, but instead I had to do the dishes. He would have gotten laid if asking once were enough. So the thought continues to rattle around my empty tired head. What would life look like?

My blood pressure would be a thing of beauty, that's for sure. I would probably lose less hair and have fewer wrinkle lines. The hair that remains on my head probably wouldn't be gray and frizzy. I would look rested and rejuvenated. I would wake up in the morning and perhaps put on something besides my Mom uniform, which is worn out yoga pants and a stained t-shirt.

This line of questioning however is doing me no favors. I am positive that I am not alone in the "If Once Were Enough" Club. It is a mythical alternate universe, one that does not exist. I guarantee that if once were enough, life would be boring and mundane. If we are being honest, my kids are doing all of the things I did to my parents when I was a kid.

I remember my Mom telling me that she was going to run away so she could be left alone. She also told us that she was going to change her name to a four letter word so we could no longer scream for her. She would say "My name is now shit, so if you call my name you will be smacked in the mouth for cursing." I remember thinking how awful that was. Why on earth she would say such horrible things to her loving children? Twenty five years later I now know why she said them, and I find myself doing the same thing. My key phrase to my children is "I'm Done!" I find that I say this several times a day, and the frequency increases throughout the week. I was talking with a friend of mine in front of our kid's school today and she is also a card carrying member of the "I'm Done" Club. I have a feeling that there are millions of us out there. Saturday, marked the fiftieth time I said "I'm Done" this week.

I woke up to the television blaring an awful cartoon theme song and asked the kids to turn it down. After six requests I jumped up and went into the living room to turn it down myself. I found a blanket and pillow fort that could rival the pyramids. They had moved all of the kitchen chairs into the living room and gotten every piece of fabric we owned to build this monstrosity. It wasn't even eight o'clock in the morning and I was already done. "Are you guys serious?" I asked. "What? We didn't want to wake you up to ask" was the response. I turned and walked back into my bedroom to try and center myself, as to avoid beginning the day with a series of flip flop beatings.

Later that afternoon we went out to run some errands. We went from Wal-Mart to Target where we made three separate stops to use the public restroom. We then proceeded to the grocery store to pick up something for dinner. I asked my seven year old and my five year old to sit in the cart so I could move quickly through the store. They did not want to sit next to each other in the cart and as I went to pick up my daughter she pretended to be a limp noodle. If playing dead was an Olympic sport she would be wearing gold. She instantaneously becomes sixty five pounds of pure pain in the ass. As I was standing there cursing under my breath I quietly whispered to her, "I'm Done, get in the cart."

We left Publix and stopped at Subway to pick up lunch. Once again I find myself in a public restroom with the kids. I asked each to wash their hands but the youngest one kept pushing the soap dispenser until there was a pool of soap on the floor. I grabbed his hand and rinsed it. I pulled a piece of paper towel and handed it to him so he could clean up the mess. Once he was finished I took the paper towel to throw it out. "I want to throw it out!" He shouted. My reply, "Let me do it please we need to go." That was the beginning of the end. He threw himself to the floor, in the public bathroom mind you, and began to scream as though I was poking him with scalding hot iron rods. I picked him up and walked him through Subway to order the sandwiches. He began to wail and moan like he was being scalped. I knelt down and whispered "You need to stop. I'm Done."

We made it home and started the bed time routine. I sent all three kids into the shower at the same time because I was prepping for dinner. I heard the water turn on and for about five minutes it was relatively quiet, then the screaming began. I ran in to see who had been attacked by a bear and found all three kids covered in bubble bath and spraying each other with the shower head. WTF! There were bubbles everywhere and the bathroom floor was soaked. This marked the 50th time I WAS DONE this week. This event proved to me that my kids know that I am full of shit. They know by my current track record that even though I say "I'm Done", I continue to live here and take care of them. They continue to be fed and clothed each day, and I continue to drive the Mom-mobile to school each morning.

Done does not exist. Done is nowhere near my zip code. As Moms we never get to be done. We get to be tired. We get to be sad. We get to be overwhelmed, but we NEVER get to be done. So we scoop. We scoop the bath time and bed time poop. We scoop the sibling rivalry poop, and we keep going.

What my kids *can* agree on is that they want to make me crazy with their public-shitting tendencies. I can safely say that I have gone number two in a public bathroom only a few times in my life. I hate public restrooms. They are filthy and riddled with germs and bacteria. I would always wait to go home and enjoy the safety of my porcelain throne, away from the amebic dysentery that could jump on my pant leg in the restroom at a Burger King. I always had control over where and when I wanted to use the bathroom. That was, until I had kids. If I had to go bad enough, I could leave and go home, or I could old it and suffer the prairie-dogging effects and stomach pains. I understand that some people are public poopers, but that is not my choice. I choose to hold my load for private dumping. My views on public pooping have only gotten worse since having children.

I can vividly remember the first time I had to take my first-born to a public restroom to take a shit. He was only fifteen months old. I was scared to death to take him to the restroom. Having a public restroom phobia, I was a good first time Mom who was fully prepared with one of those portable potty seats that fits right into the toilet. I had time to sanitize the seat, the toilet, the grab bar, and I eagerly waited for him to go. We were at Target, since their bathrooms are usually very clean, and of course I used the handicapped stall so I had plenty of room to stand in there with him. He went about his business and I was pleased with the results. Maybe my fears of public pooping were irrational. Public pooping wasn't so bad. Target was a safe bathroom and I had all the proper equipment for an effective mission. Perhaps I had misjudged public poopers.

Now, let's skip ahead a few years to having two children that needed to use the bathroom at the same time. Child number one and child number two both needed to go number TWO. We were on a road trip to Lego Land, and were in the middle of nowhere on a backwoods road. We came up to a Citgo station and quickly parked. Both kids were crying that they couldn't hold the shit demons in any longer. I jumped out of the van and I ran into the gas station with both poop filled toddlers in my arms. We approached the bathroom door, and the smell hit me like a ton of bricks. I opened the door and it was like a scene out of a horror movie. There was shit and piss on the floor, a condom machine on the wall, and only a roll of paper towels. I no longer had my nifty portable potty seat. I put down child number one and asked him to hold onto my leg for dear life and not to touch anything. I tried to clean off the toilet seat and line it with paper towel so child number two could sit and do a number two. As soon as I put her on the toilet she reached down and touched the seat! "STOP! DON'T TOUCH ANYTHING!!" I screamed like a lunatic. Once she finished, I swapped out the paper towel and put child number one on the toilet. As he was grunting and pushing, child number two decided to leave the safety of my leg and tried to put a penny she found on the floor into the condom machine. "Candy, Mommy?" she cried as she tried to place the filthy penny into the coin slot of the "raincoat" dispenser. I was right. Public pooping is like war. I almost didn't survive this battle.

Moving on a few more years down the road…..We were out to dinner at a restaurant with the entire family. As usual we ordered the kids meals first so they could shove food in their pie holes and stay calm until our food got to the table. Just as my dinner was placed in front of me I heard those four awful words….."I have to go" stated my middle child, "Me too" chimed in number three. "Can you guys wait?" I asked, hoping that a miracle would occur and we would make it home to avoid bathroom hell fire. No such luck. I got up from the table and escorted the two poop shooters into the restroom. I placed child number two in the stall next to us as child three and I occupied the handicap stall. I did my best to clean the seat and set him up so he didn't touch anything. He is a marathon pooper and can take upwards of 10-15 minutes to finish the project. Once completed, he jumped off the toilet and proceeded to tell me the names of the turds. He likes to name his feces. What can I say? So before I flushed he said, "Bye Dad, bye Mom", and so on. As we exited the stall to wash our hands I saw my daughter standing at the door. "Did you wash your hands?" I asked. "No" she states. "Well, did you poop?" I asked. "Yes I pooped, but I didn't wipe, so I don't have to wash my hands." WTF? Are you kidding me? I stood there in awe, speechless, but also hungry. "Wash your hands" I stated and we went back to the table. What is one more pair of shit stained underwear to wash? The war rages on.

It seems like every time we leave the house someone has to take a shit. I am not sure why anyone would want to use a public restroom. As I stated before, they are the epitome of nastiness, and I do everything that I can to steer clear of them. All three of my kids are equipped with poop-dar; it is a radar-like ability that can detect every public bathroom within a five-mile radius. Unfortunately for me, my three kids think that a public restroom is a playground. They want to stop at each one that we see. They swing from the doors, play with the locks, touch the toilet seats, and wrap toilet paper around their heads like Egyptian mummies. I have thousands of dollars' worth of toys at my house, yet a public bathroom is more appealing to these tiny turds. I am looking forward to the day when I can return my frequent public-pooper card. I am a firm believer in private pooping and I will throw a freaking party when all of my kids can go to the bathroom on their own.

The job of a parent is never ending. We have to remember to give ourselves a break. If we need to hide in our closets to gain some composure, we should do that. Moms need a time out also. We need to be able to continue to scoop the poop, and that means that we need to find our composure. I spend tons of time in my closet hiding under my desk. My closet is my office, so yes I have a desk in there. I will sit and hide and count to ten. I whisper "Serenity now", and I try to find the shreds of sanity that remain. The days are long and I can't scoop all of the poop at the same time. None of us can. No one's shovel is big enough for that.

Parenting is hard enough when things are going well. It can become unmanageable when things go south. My youngest son was born with brain damage. He suffered a birth injury and it caused some issues with motor, cognitive, and behavioral development. I will never forget the day he was diagnosed with autism.

I didn't talk to anyone about his diagnosis outside of my husband for the first week. I was angry. I was sad. I was worried. I was every emotion you could think of and I still had to keep going. I wanted to run away and hide. I wanted to put my hands on my sons head and wish it away. I wanted to fix him. I was hoping that by keeping it a secret, it wasn't really happening. If we could just be still and quiet it would all be OK. But that wasn't the case. We had to move forward. We had to get a game plan. We had to talk about it.

This was more than just Mom or kid poop. This was serious *life* poop that I had to process on his five year old behalf. After I let everything process, I sat down and I wrote this letter to my son:

To my baby,

I love you. You get to be the baby forever. We knew the day that you were born that something was different about you. The doctor was late and I was told to wait. We waited a bit too long. We didn't know it for the first year, but your tiny brain went a while without oxygen. It caused some brain damage and we still aren't sure exactly what that means for you in the long run. The cerebral palsy caused your left leg and arm to move a little differently from the right side, but they get the job done. I can see how smart you are, there is no hiding that. It might take you longer to solve the problem, but I know you can do it. You amaze me every single day.

You are one of the funniest people I know, and I'm pretty funny if I do say so myself. You make me laugh each and every day. I also cry almost every day. I cry because it isn't fair. I cry because I lose my temper. I cry because I am exhausted. I cry because I just want you to be "normal." I cry because you don't sleep, and I need you to sleep. I cry because you still aren't potty trained and you are the only kid in your class that wears a diaper at nap time. I cry because my heart hurts for you.

This past week I took you to the doctor and they confirmed that you also have autism. Just like I knew that something wasn't right before, I knew that this was also a possibility. It didn't make it any easier to hear. I cried when I took you home from the doctor's office. You asked me what was wrong. I couldn't reply.

I know that you are exactly who you were meant to be. I cry because I don't always know how to help you. I cry because I can't find the patience to give you exactly what you need. I cry because I fear that you are broken and I don't know how to fix you. I cry because life is hard enough when you are "normal."

I know that you are happy most of the time. I know that you love me all of the time. Please know that I love you too. I love you even when I am sad, and even when I cry. I love you when I yell and when I say things like, "I am on my last nerve" and "I am done". I will do whatever I can for you, no matter what that looks like.

You have a beautiful soul. I try very hard to remember that when you are kicking and screaming: when we are in public and I have to leave the store or the restaurant because the meltdown is a level ten. I cry when you hit me, or your brother or sister. When you scream and cry and I just can't figure out what set you off. I try. I promise you that I will always try.

You are not your brain damage. You are not your autism. You are my son. You are a comedian. You are a boy full of energy and ideas. You are my shadow. I love every piece of you. I cannot fix you because you are not broken. You are a puzzle that was put together with a different method. It's my job care for you and love you just the way you are. Perfectly imperfect, just like the rest of us.

I published this on my blog and it was very freeing. I had so many Moms write to me to talk about autism and how it affects their families. It showed me the power that a community like ours can create. I was overwhelmed with so many people reaching out to me to talk about their children and how I wasn't alone. I knew that I didn't need to keep his diagnosis a secret. It is part of who he is. It is not what defines him, but it is part of his story.

No matter what is wrong with our children, as parents we want to fix it. We want to wave the magic wand and make them all better. We scoop for our children. We scoop to let them know that it will all be OK. We scoop so we can survive the moments when a doctor tells us that there is something "different" about our children. As parents we will scoop anything for our children. I think the parent pooper scooper is the biggest and most important scooper of them all.

Mom poop is powerful poop. As Moms we want to do everything for our children. We want to make them happy, we want to give them the world. We want them to have the best experience in every situation. That is not reality. That is not what is best for our children. They need to struggle. They need to learn to survive. They need to learn to scoop their own poop from time to time. If we scoop all of our poop and all of their poop, the scooper will over flow and the poop ends up back on the floor. As Moms we need to know when it is not our job to scoop our children's poop. I am not perfect, and I still scoop poop that, rightfully, my kids should be learning to scoop for themselves. It is a work in progress. We are a work in progress. We are all learning. Poop scooping is hard to teach, and even harder to learn.

5. HOUSE POOP

Let's rewind for a minute. Let's go back to a time when I was on top of things. I used to have a clean house. I used to have people over to my home and not worry when they sat down at my kitchen table. I would run through the house sweeping and fluffing pillows. I would check to make sure picture frames were straight and spray each room with Lysol and air freshener. I would worry about someone coming over for two days prior to them actually setting foot in my house, but I would open my door when they arrived and be ready for their visit. They would enter into a clean house with vacuum lines in the carpet.

I distinctly remember when that all changed. The holiday season of 2009 was a doozy. It was my daughter's first Christmas. She was an adorable 10 month old, and my son was a super excited almost three year old big boy.

To say that my role in the family was demanding would be an understatement. I decided to go to my family physician and tell him about my woes. I was burnt out, overwhelmed and on top of that, I was training for a half marathon. I remember sitting in her office crying and explaining that I couldn't figure out how to keep it all together. I was tired, over worked, and felt defeated. She offered me a short term solution of "Happy Pills." I didn't think it was a great idea to take medication; I felt like that was admitting I had a problem. I talked with my husband and we decided I should give them a try. I filled the prescription and went on my way.

December was blissful. I was calm, relaxed, and had my head above water. My husband and I had been discussing our family situation and with one boy and one girl, we decided that we were finished having children. We were all set. I called the OBGYN to schedule an appointment for a tubal ligation. My husband claimed that he could not have a vasectomy because there was a risk that he would not be able to perform the same in the bedroom. I told him that was complete and utter bull shit, but there was no way he was going to let anyone near his eggplant with a scalpel in their hand.

I felt like a rock star mom and wife. We made it through the holiday season unscathed. I kept thinking to myself "I am the BEST MOM EVER! Look at how awesome I am!"

By January, I had gotten my life together and I decided to stop taking the "Happy Pills". They seemed to be detrimental in the boudoir, and I wasn't having any of that. I started planning my daughter's first birthday. It was a blast. The whole family got together. Later that month my husband and I had a date night. We went to a work event where he was recognized as employee of the month. It was so nice to be out and away from it all. When the bartender asked, " Two for one?" I exclaimed "YES!" It wasn't really a question was it? I am away from my kids. I was looking hot, all dressed up and ready to go. I will never forget this night. We ate, drank, and found ourselves drunkenly entwined on the couch with reckless abandon.

January led to February and life was flying by at a mile a minute. Between work and kids, my life was crazy. I had my annual OBGYN apt the week of Valentine's Day. How romantic, "May I check your cervix?" Another question that I deem rhetorical, much like two for one drinks. Same old routine; pee in this cup. Sit in this room. Get naked. Put on this paper towel gown and try not to look awkward while lying back with your ankle's by your ears.

I began to explain to my doctor that I was done having children and ready to have a tubal. At that point the nurse came in a looked at the doctor. I looked at them both and he said one word that I will never forget, "Congratulations!" I replied, "What? Congratulations on what?" I thought to myself did I win a free pap smear? He continued, "Congratulations. You're pregnant." I sat there stunned and sedated, much like deer caught in the sight line of the hunter. Frozen.

"Pregnant? No, I'm not pregnant. I need to get my tubes tied." I stated. The doctor just looked at me and explained that it was in fact true, I was pregnant.

I now had to take this information home to my husband. It went over like a fart in Church. I'm pretty sure at one point he said "NO!" I began to cry while talking with him. I continued to cry for about three months. That Mom of the year who had it all together two months ago was fading away. Reality sank in and I realized that I would have two children in diapers.

But I digress. The third blessing arrived in October. I never got to run that half marathon, but I did run like a cheetah six weeks after he was born; I ran to finally get that tubal.

Now, with three children running around my home, I know that anytime someone sits at my kitchen table, they will undoubtedly sit in maple syrup, pieces of a granola bar, or some other sticky solution that remains behind after the dinner dishes have been cleared. I do my best. I wipe down the table. I dust off the chairs. I even got a dog to eat the crumbs that fall to the floor. We live in our home and it looks, "Lived in." We host back yard BBQ's, and have family over as often as we can. I leave piles of laundry on the couch for days at a time, and I never seem to get all of the dishes done before bed. I choose to let the house poop pile up to a certain extent. I can only scoop so much laundry poop each day. My kids never go to school in dirty clothes. Wait. Strike that. My kids only go to school in dirty clothes because they chose to, not because there wasn't a clean alternative.

If cleaning the house every day so it looks like no one lives there is someone's thing, that person can scoop that house poop like a boss. If that makes people happy and keeps their Zen in check, great. What is important is that if it is not our thing, we should let it go. We should not overflow our scoopers with poop that doesn't need to be scooped right then and there.

I do laundry every day, but I do not fold laundry every day. I scoop a little bit when I can, where I can, but I don't let Mount Laundry dictate my life any longer. There will be laundry to do until the day that I die. I refuse to fight a losing battle. Instead I choose to only scoop what I can tolerate on any given day. I guarantee that if people came over to my house they would find a laundry basket full of clean folded laundry. That basket never gets put away. I used to hate the basket because it was a reminder that I had something to do. Now, I welcome the basket, because it means we are still alive. We are all still stinking up the undies so they need to hit the washing machine.

Part of married life with children is the daily grind of chores, not just tackling Mount Laundry, but also grocery shopping. It is, in fact, a necessary evil. We need food to survive; therefore we must go out and purchase the food. While at the grocery store a while back, I began unloading my items onto the conveyor belt. The bag boy politely asked, "Paper or plastic?" As I answered his question I saw the cashier out of the corner of my eye. She had a somewhat shocked look on her face. I didn't pay much attention to her because I was battling with my children over who was going to place the items on the belt. One kid was under the basket, one was standing in the basket helping me unload, and the third was reading Soap Opera Digest.

When I go shopping, I don't just pick up a few things. My cart usually looks like I am preparing for the Apocalypse. Living in a house with five people causes me to buy a variety of items. It is not uncommon to see all or some combination of the following items in my cart; diapers, beer, wine, panty liners, bathroom wipes, lubricant, anti-acid medication, anti-diarrhea medication, anti-itch cream, drain cleaner, batteries, lighters, rubbing alcohol, and sometimes hemorrhoid cream.

I have never paid much attention to how I unload the cart. I am usually trying to keep my kids from stealing candy or scanning the cart to remember what item I had forgotten. Before having children I would get embarrassed if the cashier saw me buying condoms and beer, or panty liners and bathroom wipes. I would hide the items under other things, perhaps a magazine or spread them out as to look less conspicuous. When the cashier picks up the magazine and sees the condoms, I am pretty sure she doesn't think I am going home to have a water balloon fight. I am at the point where I refuse to be embarrassed for buying personal items. If I am buying beer and condoms together, it just means I'm going to have a good time and I'm not stupid enough to drink without protection. I know what happens after I have a few beers, and I am in no way interested in having another child.

When I got home and began to unload the groceries, I figured out the puzzled look on my cashiers face. I finished unloading everything and found one lonely brown paper bag . When I opened it I saw the following items: lubricant, batteries, and a bottle of wine. I assumed at that point that the cashier thought I would be using those items together. To be honest the batteries were for my son's remote control car, however I give the girl points for imagination.

It made me stop and think about the judging eyes of my cashier. We have all had a cashier give us a dirty look from time to time. Perhaps when we run into the store with your kids to buy beer and diapers. Why do they look at us with such disdain? I can't have a beer while diapering my child? It's not like I came into the store drunk with my children and bought more beer and forgot the diapers; now that is a reason to give a dirty look.

So from now on I will make sure and tell the cashier what I will be doing with all of the items from my cart. "The lubricant is for me and my husband. I need the panty liners because I gave birth to three kids and I pee my pants when I sneeze. I have children with allergies and need creams, ointment and disinfectants. We are very hairy people and the drains get clogged all the time, so drain cleaner is a must have item. I have frequent heartburn and three children-sized hemorrhoids, so I need a lot of anti-acids and hemorrhoid cream. I need a lighter because I love to light candles, and I need the batteries for my vibrator. Plastic bags will be fine, thanks."

At thirty six years old I refuse to accept any shame or judgement from a cashier, or anyone else who has something to say about my grocery store purchases.

Life is too short to hide the lubricant and batteries. I am also too tired to normally notice that someone is sending me a judgmental glare. Being a parent comes with a chronic state of exhaustion.

I remember a Monday morning not too long ago after a particularly exhausting weekend. I looked down and saw my gas light glowing like Christmas morning. Awesome. I was on my way to drop the kids at school, and as usual we would be late. I haven't been on time for anything in the past ten years. I honestly can't remember an event where I was first to arrive. I pulled into the gas station and jumped out of the van to fill up the Hot Mom Machine. I swiped my credit card and it gave me a very simple command. "Please enter zip code." I sat there for thirty seconds frozen with fear. It appeared that I had excessively early onset Alzheimer's. I had no freaking clue what my zip code was. I mean, I have lived in the same town my entire life. I began to recite my address and still to no avail. What was happening to me? Why couldn't I remember my zip code? I looked into the van, and I saw the culprits. Three small brain-washers, sitting with lunch boxes and backpacks.

Finally, after five minutes of brain cell hide and seek, it came to me and I entered the numbers. I stood there in utter disbelief. Why was it so hard to complete daily tasks that shouldn't have taken even an ounce of brain power? I got back into the Mini and turned on the radio.

Ten year old: Mom, put on what does the Fox Say.

Me: No, I cannot listen to that song one more time.

Ten year old: *Inhaled breath, gearing up to argue back*

Me: We all know what the fox is going to say. He says the same thing every time we listen to the song.

Those Swedish Sons of Bitches have made my radio life a living hell for over a year now. Damn geniuses.

I pulled into the drop off-line and parked. Out went two of the three master-minds and I was on my way with the third child. After everyone was safely at school I began my trek home to perform the tasks ahead of me; my mind still wondering where the zip code I had known for so many years had disappeared to. As I pulled into my driveway it hit me. I had hit rock bottom of sleep deprivation. I couldn't remember the last time I had eight hours of consecutive sleep.

It has been a decade since I went to bed and woke up refreshed and ready to conquer the day. I sat sad and still for a moment. I knew why I hadn't slept in years. I can't solely blame the poop machines, but they are a big part of it. Three kids in a queen size bed is a math problem that cannot be solved. One Miniature schnauzer and a husband that snores add to the equation. Shopping lists that run through my mind at two thirty in the morning, and getting up to pee at least once will demolish any respite. These are common problems of any mother. But this led me to a very interesting question. What could I do if I had eight consecutive hours of sleep?

This was a very fascinating thought. Would it be possible to have every load of laundry done? Would dirty dishes in the sink be a thing of the past? Would I be P.T.O. President of my kid's school? No, forget that! I would be President of the United States. Watch out POTUS. With eight hours of consecutive sleep I would rule over the land. I would be unstoppable. Just think. It would be amazing. I could sit in that Oval Office ordering around my constituents', demanding change. I would be passing laws left and right stating that Fathers are required to get up in the middle of the night and change diapers and get the 19th glass of water. Perhaps I have watched too many "House of Cards" episodes. No, I don't think I will enter a life of politics, but I will fantasize about those precious hours of sleep that evade me.

In reality I have no idea what my day would look like with eight hours of sleep under my belt. I am not sure once we become parents if that it is even possible. I do know that at the end of the day I am the good kind of tired; the kind of tired that comes from productivity and a sense of accomplishment.

As exhausting as house poop can be, determining which poop is the most important to scoop it vital. It is not physically possible for anyone to get it all done each and every day. I choose not to scoop the laundry poop each day. Others might choose to let the dishes sit in the sink, or never wash a window. We are not bad Moms because we only vacuum once a week. In fact, we will be less stressed Moms if we choose to prioritize our poop and scoop what needs to be done so we can focus on more important poop.

If we actively prioritize our poop we will feel better at the end of the day. Remember that our priorities will not necessarily align with others' priorities. As a household we will need to set the priorities. We should sit with our spouses and determine what is most important, determine what we can and cannot live with, and find the middle ground, because team work is required.

This did not happen in my house overnight. My husband and I both work, but he was not someone who helped with the house work. He rarely did the dishes, and to date he has never cleaned a toilet. It took years of fighting and conversations for us to find the middle ground.

6. MARRIAGE POOP

I am one of the really lucky ones. I married my best friend. I met my husband at the age of fifteen. We both played soccer at our local high school. We dated through high school. We dated on and off throughout college. We did the whole I hate you, I love you thing. No matter what was going on in my life, he was in my heart.

We got married in 2003. I was twenty three, he was twenty four. We were ready to conquer the world. We were both substitute teachers at the time, making eight dollars an hour to "teach" high school students who were only a few years younger than we were. We bought our first home, a tiny condo, that we decorated with garage sale furniture and paint from the local Walmart. I think I painted the entire condo with one gallon of paint. Yellow paint. Very ugly yellow paint. We were young, stupid, and in love.

Fast forward to 2005. I wanted a baby. I needed to have a baby. I was wise and ready at twenty five and I needed him to get on board with the idea that we were going to be parents.

Business Manager: We are broke. We do not need to have kids right now.

Me: I want to have a baby *now*.

Business Manager: Let's wait. Let's be smart.

Me: I *am* ready. We are ready. There will never be enough money or time.

We did this for a few months. He bought me a dog to quench my baby thirst, but it didn't last long. I broke him down and we began "trying" to have a baby. I became pregnant after a few months. I was so excited. I was going to be a Mom. I had always wanted to be a Mom. A few weeks later, I called my husband at work to tell him I was bleeding, and after a doctor's visit, we were told that I had miscarried the baby.

I was crushed. I felt that I had failed at being a Mom. I couldn't' get it right. I was a mess. I cried for about a week. I'm sure he was devastated as well, but to be honest, I was only thinking about the baby that "I" had lost. I felt alone. After a few months we tried again. Again we got pregnant after a few months. I was nervous. What was going to happen? Would the baby be okay? Again, I miscarried. I fell into a dark place. It was uncomfortable to talk to anyone about what was going on. I cried a lot. He didn't know what to say. We pretty much just existed. We decided to take a break from "trying." We met with a few doctors and they all explained that this was common and not to worry. That was not helpful in the least. I didn't want to hear that it was common, or that I was normal. I wanted a baby. I wanted to be able to have a baby. I wanted to be able to make my husband a Father.

The third time was a charm. After a long, scary, pregnancy, that included a surgery, medications, and three months of bed rest, we welcomed our son in 2006. He was amazing. He was our gift from God. When they handed him to me, it was like I had already known him forever. He was a piece of my soul in tiny human form. I remember turning to look at my husband and falling in love with him all over again. He was going to be the best Dad ever.

I had no idea that after taking the baby home I would quickly feel like I was losing my mind. It was like having an angry houseguest who wouldn't leave. The baby cried all the time. The only time he didn't cry was when he was feeding, and let me tell you, breastfeeding was extremely difficult to figure out. Having a baby with colic was miserable. He cried and cried and cried. I don't think I slept for the first six months. That new overwhelming love that I found for my husband quickly dwindled, and I would day dream about slapping him in the face with a 2x4. He got to leave and go to work while I stayed home with a crying baby whose only goal in life was to rob me of sleep. I had a severe case of "Mom Guilt."

I am positive that all first time Moms suffer from this at one time or another. It took me years to manage and let go of the Mom guilt. It took me years to realize that I was the one who was in fact allowing the guilt to remain a companion in my life.

Having learned from my mistakes, here is my advice on surviving the first days with a baby:

SLEEP: This title is in capital letters because it is simply that important. Sleep as often as possible. If someone offers to sit with the baby, tell them yes please, and then go take a nap. Don't do laundry, or dishes, or anything else. Sleep is so important and although we can live without it, we don't function well and everyone suffers.

Breast or Bottle: This is 100% up to you. It is your body, and here is the best part....there is no wrong answer. You will in fact be feeding your baby, so either way you are doing your job. I have done both and I can tell you that all three of my kids are alive and thriving at the ages of ten, seven, and five. They all took some from the boob, and the rest from the bottle. It is up to you and you alone to decide.

Eat: Don't forget to feed yourself. Eat what you want, when you want. You need to have enough energy to take care of all of the people living in your tiny village. Keep up your energy and don't even think about "losing the baby weight" at this point in time. You will need all of the energy that you can produce to not only physically take care of baby, but also to function mentally as a human.

Accept Help: You are home with your miracle and he hasn't stopped crying for a solid hour, if your mother in law or best friend just so happened to stop by, pass that baby over. Take a shower, a nap, or paint your toenails. Take a deep breath and know that it's okay to accept help and take a break. You are a better Mom when you accept help. The more the merrier.

Give up the Guilt: Mom guilt is self-imposed. It is pretty much the same thing as the Boogie-Man. We all know that the Boogie-Man isn't real, but tell that to a three year-old who insists that he is in his closet. Mom guilt can only wreck us if we allow it to become part of us. For many years I struggled with this daunting guilt. It is not productive or realistic to think that I will be able to be everything all of the time. Let the dishes sit, the laundry pile up, and the toys remain on the floor. I guarantee that they will still need attention tomorrow, so sit in a rocking chair with your baby and be still.

Cry: It feels good to let it out. Crying is an acceptable emotional outlet, especially if you just gave birth to a baby. Crying will give you an outlet and help you feel better about the current situation, even if your crying about an ASPCA commercial. I get it. I have done it. I will most likely do it again.

So let yourself adjust to having another person in the house. When my first born was two weeks old I called my mother and cried for at least an hour. He was a colicky baby who only wanted to nurse. I remember telling her, "He is like an angry house guest that won't leave. I know I am supposed to love him, but he just cries all the time." As soon as the words left my mouth I felt bad, but what my Mom said I will never forget. "He won't cry forever. Give him to your husband and go take a shower."

My Mom was right, the crying eventually stopped, and then I had more babies. Two more babies to be accurate. Becoming parents creates a lot of poop. Physical poop, like projectile poop that shoots across the room at lightning speed, and metaphorical poop, like Mom guilt. Whether we are cleaning poop off of a wall, or dealing with the stress that Mom guilt causes, it can be extremely difficult to scoop the poop.

Finding balance in a marriage is imperative and it directly correlates to how well we scoop our marriage poop. In my home I normally do all of the shopping for our household. I asked my husband to go to the store for me. Around noon, I sent him to the store for a total of five items. One of the items on the list was panty liners. After giving birth to three children, I need the type of protection that a maximum protection panty liner provides. It is not a fun topic to discuss, but it is my lot in life to pee when I sneeze, laugh, jump, trip, fall, high-five, or basically exist.

I was very specific with the type of panty liner and brand that I wanted him to buy. I am a creature of habit, so I like to purchase the same product when I get great results. Panty liners are a product that need to work...EVERY TIME. My husband sent me a text stating that he could not find the brand that I wanted.

I told him where they were located in the store, and asked him to find a store employee if he couldn't find them. I knew that when I told him to ask someone that he wouldn't. If he won't stop to ask for directions, why on earth would he ask a store associate where the "pee pads" are located in the store. My guess is that he figured if he asked an associate they would naturally assume that the panty liners were for him. I mean what other logical thought would the associate have. A man in the feminine hygiene aisle, he must be shopping for his own personal use.

Ten minutes later, he texted back stating that they really don't have them and he sent me a picture of the brands that they did have. I looked over the selection and asked him to pick up the box of Always brand panty liners and check to see if they were un-scented. He spent another five minutes reading the box. My guess is that he ran from the feminine care aisle and attempted to hide in the corner of the store. We had been married for over twelve years at that point. He has watched me give birth three times, and yet he was embarrassed to buy a feminine care product. He finally texted me back stating that he didn't think they were scented.

I found it necessary to screw with him at this point. Below is our short and sweet text conversation:

I couldn't help but have a little fun with my husband. I mean seriously, it is not that big a deal. I wasn't asking him to go up to a woman in the aisle and ask her for a detailed personal review on the panty liner. I just wanted him to get the right ones.

He apparently didn't think my joke was funny. I still laugh when I see the picture that I took of our text conversation. Life is too short to be embarrassed over panty liners and personal hygiene products. I can safely say that I wouldn't have a problem going to the store to buy him jock itch cream. He did come home with a pack of panty liners, so it was a successful venture.

Married people are required to scoop the other spouse's poop. In this case, he was actually scooping my pee, which is crass and gross, but it is part of being married. So he took one for the team that day and scooped the poop. I was appreciative.

Years earlier I had to scoop his poop. We were newlyweds, maybe married for just over a year. My husband woke up sick. Not "Man cold" sick. Really sick. We thought it was an awful stomach flu, but after he progressively got worse we went to the emergency room. It was in fact his appendix. It had ruptured and it was leaking fluid into his abdomen. He was rushed back to emergency surgery. I had never been so nervous in my life. What if he died on the table. What if there were complications? What if?

After a few hours, the surgeon came out and addressed his Mom first, and then me. Par for the course. I was taken back to see him and he looked so sad. He was in fact fine, but seeing him in a hospital bed was a very unnerving sight. I stayed with him for two days, like a wonderful doting wife. I like to think back and remember being pleasant and loving towards him, but that probably wasn't true. I'm sure I was snippy and snarky, which is my true inner beauty. The nurse came in and explained that my husband would need to do a number two prior to his release from the hospital. She explained that she was going to need to "get" him to go. She showed him the suppository and said, "I can do it, or she can do it" pointing at me. My eyes were as big as saucers. Me? Why on earth would I do that? My husband turned and looked at the nurse and said, "She will do it."

I was handed a medical grade examination glove, a tube of lubricant, and the suppository. I did the deed. I mentally blocked out most of it, but I got the job done. Later that evening I walked past the nurses station and one of the nurses look at me and said with a smile, "You are a great girlfriend to help him out like that." I cocked my head to the side and said, "If I was his girlfriend, you can bet your sweet ass I wouldn't have stuck my finger up his butt. That's my husband. I had to."

We all do things in marriage that we don't want to do. I can guarantee that when Business Manager reads this portion of the book he will want it deleted, and I will have to remind him that I helped him poop back in 2004.

Marriage poop can be very sticky poop. In July of 2015 I had my first viral post. I woke up that morning and checked out the trending news like I do every day. I noticed that a company named Ashley Madison had been hacked. What was interesting about the hack was that the company was a dating website for married people. I had no idea that married people dated. I think I would be rather perturbed if I found out that my husband was dating. Below is my first viral post about married dating:

<u>Life is Short, Have an Affair</u>

Earlier this week my four year old said something really funny in the car. He called my husband a "kissey face" and said that Daddy kisses everyone in town. I said, "What? Who did you see Daddy kiss?" He replied, "I was just tricking you. He only kisses you." After the minor cardio infarction that I suffered, my husband and I had a conversation about cheating. He said, "How do people who live in a small town have an affair? I mean, everyone knows that you're married. I just don't get it."

Maybe they have an account on Ashley Madison? Have you heard of this website? I hadn't, but today I saw that Ashley Madison was hacked and it's 37 million members are in danger of having their identities leaked. Yes, you heard correctly, 37 MILLION MEMBERS. This dating website is for married people to meet up and have affairs with other married people.

Below is the Ashley Madison website information:

~*Ashley Madison is the most famous name in infidelity and married dating. As seen on Hannity, Howard Stern, TIME, BusinessWeek, Sports Illustrated, Maxim, USA Today. Ashley Madison is the most recognized and reputable married dating company. Our Married Dating Services for Married individuals Work. Ashley Madison is the most successful website for finding an affair and cheating partners. Have an Affair today on Ashley Madison. Thousands of cheating wives and cheating husbands signup everyday looking for an affair. We are the most famous website for discreet encounters between married individuals. Married Dating has never been easier. With Our affair guarantee package we guarantee you will find the perfect affair partner. Sign up for Free today.*

Now that you have read this, do you have any questions? I did. Here are a list of the questions and thoughts that came to mind after reading about this company and the current security breach.

1. WTF? Is this for real?

2. No seriously, is this a real thing?

3. 37 Million people use this? Do these people have jobs?

4. If you're married, and have a job, where the hell do you find the time for a dating website?

5. I am really confused. 37 Million people?

6. If life is short, shouldn't you love the one you're with? You know, the one you married?

7. Who is going to be liable for all of the murders that occur when the 37 million members information is leaked?

8. I hope John Bobbitt isn't a member. He didn't do so well after the last time he got caught.

9. I bet divorce attorneys love to advertise on this site.

10. If you're married, aren't you supposed to be

monogamous? Am I thinking of something else?

11. You probably need to be really organized to cheat. I can't remember where I put my car keys. I would get caught in like 5 minutes.

12. Married dating is a thing? If you're married, why are you dating?

13. I am really having a difficult time with this.

14. This is the most reputable married dating company? There are more? Oh Dear Lord!

15. This website has a guarantee? How can you guarantee you will find the perfect affair partner?

16. This is a rabbit hole. I need to stop.

I am very interested to see how this security breach plays out. I am also baffled at the fact that 37 million married people are members of an online dating service. I guess monogamy is a thing of the past. Perhaps we are on the verge of a new definition of marriage. Maybe instead of saying "I do" people should say, "I'll try, but when I get bored, I'll try something else." Because life is short. Have an affair.

I have known the Business Manager longer than I haven't known him, and we are still going strong. Luckily we are both too exhausted to "married date" so the Business Manager and I will hang in there. It can be hard to keep a marriage fresh after thirteen years and three kids.

Sex is an important part of marriage. I am not a marriage therapist, but if there is not intimacy between spouses, the relationship turns into a roommate situation; the couple lives side by side, but is missing the connection.

The sex changes after the nuptials. Sex changes *again* after the arrival of babies.

Here are 11 types of sex that people who are "married with children" have:

"Shower" Sex: It's not steamy, hot, sudsy, porn shower sex. It's more like; "Hey, we have ten minutes and I don't want to have to shower again today, so do want to do it?" shower sex. One partner most likely ends up smacking his or her head into the shower door or wall, and at least once during the sex a kid will knock on the bathroom door and ask, "Why are you both in there?"

"Hotel" Sex: Oh yeah. Married people love hotel sex, but not for the obvious reason. Hotel sex means being away from the kids and away from any interruptions. Which in turn means after the five minutes the sex takes, it is possible to take a three hour uninterrupted nap. That's right, a sexy nap that will leave anyone completely satisfied.

"Are you serious?" Sex: This type of sex usually occurs when one person is in the mood and the other one just wants to go to bed. In my case it usually starts with my husband pretending to rub my back. Somehow he gets confused and rubs my breasts thinking they are my shoulder blades (In his defense I have very small breasts.). This usually prompts me to say, "Are you serious?" which usually ends with, "It will only take five minutes."

"Roll over on your side" Sex: This one might just be me, but when I am in the middle of an episode of Grey's Anatomy and my husband has an urge, I will be a good sport and roll over, but I always roll towards the T.V. I don't want to miss anything. Plus, Dr. Avery is a delightful milk chocolate treat that, like a Hershey bar, always leaves me satisfied.

"I'm just kidding unless you're serious" Sex: Married sex can be exciting. You can ask your partner about their fantasies and what gets their engine all revved up. Most of the time people say things to find out what type of reaction they are going to receive. So if a woman jokes about buying a vibrator and says, "I'm just kidding, unless you think it's a good idea" her husband should buy her a vibrator. Buy a bunch of stuff. Sex is fun and we need to spice it up to keep it interesting and exciting.

"10 Minutes until they get home" Sex: This usually occurs when the grandparents or someone has the kids but they are on their way home. We meant to have sex earlier, but the laundry and dishes got in the way. So we do what we have to do and get the sex and shower completed in record time.

"Did you fall asleep?" Sex: When our children are young, we have many sleepless nights. I am currently living in a constant state of exhaustion and my youngest is five years. old. I am not sure if or when I will wake from the fog, but I do know that there is a possibility that I promised my husband sex and instead I fell asleep. If other husbands are like mine, they will wake their wives up and collect on the promise.

"I've had a box of wine" Sex: Raising kids and working is stressful. On the weekends it's nice to relax and have a drink. Sometimes those drink turns into a bottle. When that happens, count on some fun drunk sex. This usually involves playful chasing and potentially a spanking. It definitely ends with an "I can't believe I drank that much" hangover in the morning.

"Did the doorknob just turn?" Sex: The fear is always there. Is tonight going to be the night that one of the kids walks in and finds Daddy wrapping Mommy up into a figure eight wrestling move? It seems that we are always listening to hear little footsteps and the turn of the doorknob. It will happen. At some point they will get an eye full, and the questions will ensue. Lock the door people. Lock the door.

"OMG! We cannot have another baby!"
Sex: I know all about this kind of sex. Life is going great. I feel like I am on top of my game, and BOOM! I get drunk at a company party and end up having unprotected couch sex and waking up saying, "We cannot have another baby. I am done having babies." nine months later, I had baby number three. Six weeks after baby number three, I had a tubal ligation.

Which leads to the final kind of sex.

"I got fixed!" Sex: This is by far the best kind of sex. No condoms. No worries. Just freedom. If one spouse is fixed, the sex can be anytime and potentially anywhere. But don't get too excited. With responsibilities, kids, and poop to scoop, the options for when and where are a bit limited. An empty bounce house at a children birthday party is not a great option. Be smart now that you no longer have to be safe.

Any, or all, of these types of sex are perfectly normal. Kids, jobs, and exhaustion can get in the way of romance and roses. We should do it when we can, as often as we can, and remember that we picked our spouses for a reason. I am hopeful that one day we can have loud, crazy, and naked all over the house sex. If we continue to scoop our marriage poop, then hopefully the varieties of sex can continue to be a reality because we will have maintained balance in our marriage.

However, when a relationship is strained, the sex can stop. It is difficult to find time for each other if one person can't stand the sight of one another. In July of 2015 my husband and I hit a wall. We were exhausted. We were overworked. We were stressed out, and we were about to have some major fireworks.

I had been working hard on the blog. I was writing, taking care of the kids, the house, the dogs, the lawn, cooking, cleaning, and oh yes, my full time job. He was on edge due to recent home renovations. We were hemorrhaging money, and living with three kids while renovating can cause anyone's blood pressure to shoot off like a NASA rocket launch. We were constantly at each other's throats. I didn't want to talk about paint colors, tile grout, or floor sealant. I was ready to put a for sale sign up in the yard and abandon the property.

I was at the point where I would look at my husband and daydream about inflicting pain on him. I would pinch my fingers together and imagine I was squeezing his head between a vice. If this is disturbing, rest assured, I did not cause him any bodily harm. I pictured it. I enjoyed thinking about it, but I never did it.

I was rushing around the house getting the kids ready for a Fourth of July party when the poop hit the fan. We began to fight about something trivial. I don't remember what it was. I looked at him and I exploded. I began to scream. I wasn't shouting, I wasn't yelling, I was SCREAMING. I was screaming so loud and so hard, that I was shaking. I was screaming about being tired. I was screaming about the dishes, the laundry, the kids, the constant projects, and the lack of sleep. I started to cry.

My husband was sitting in our red arm chair with a frozen look of fear on his face. He sat very still. I got very quiet and I went into the bathroom to get some toilet paper. (We are not tissue people. They are a waste of money, so I just use toilet paper.) I came back into the bedroom and I sat on the bed. He was still frozen. Encased in ice like Elsa. Frozen.

Me: I can't do this anymore. I can't act like I am okay. I can't live like this. *Ugly crying- face in hands*

Business Manager: What did I do?

Me: Are you serious? You have no idea what you have done? Do you live in this house?

I began to shout at him again. It apparently wasn't a fight. He had no clue why I was upset. I tried to calm myself down the best I could.

Me: I am tired of being the one who does all of the housework. I do all of the yard work. I clean the pool. I take the kids to school. I cook. I clean. I work. I write the blog. I can't stand to look at another piece of crown molding. I am tired of living in a constant mess. I can't do this any longer.

Business Manager: I help.

Me: *I laughed out loud, which did not help the mood in the room.*

Business Manager: What do you want from me?

Me: I WANT YOU TO HELP ME! I NEED HELP!!!!!

Me: *Screaming again. Crying again.*

Business Manager: I help. Sometimes I do the dishes.

Me: You *still* don't get it!

Business Manager: I know you do a lot. I work hard too. You aren't the only one who works.

Me: It's not a competition. I don't want to be the winner. I want you to know that I need your help. I need your support. I need you to know what I do all day and I need you to value that.

I needed him to know that I couldn't do it alone. I needed him to know that I was struggling. I was anything but okay. I laughed again. It wasn't on purpose. I didn't laugh to make him mad. He still didn't get it.

I started to talk to him about what my day actually looks like. From the morning, through school drop off. Coming home and starting dinner. Working, writing, shooting video, switching laundry, running outside to mow the grass, heading to the grocery store, back into the office for phone calls, and then back out the door to get the kids. I explained that once the kids are home the fighting starts, the homework starts, the stress sets in.

I had yet to stop crying. I had snot running down my face. I could hear the kids in the living room watching TV. They knew this was bad. They knew not to come to the door. I immediately felt guilty for letting them hear the words I had shouted at their Father.

Me: I have to get the kids ready. We are going to be late to the party.

Business Manager: *Looking puzzled* You are going to the party?

Me: Yes, I am done right now. I love you, but we can't finish this right now.

I left the room and got the kids ready for the party. I did my best to put on my happy face and we took the kids to listen to the second set of fireworks that day.

The fighting got better for a while. We began to wrap up most of the home renovations over the next few months. I kept working, writing, and scooping the poop. I tried being very specific with what I wanted my husband to do. I would tell him that I needed him to do the dishes so I could go back in my office, or I needed him to put the kids to bed so I could edit a video.

We were hitting September and we were almost done

with the home renovations. The floor was being laid and we were down to painting and a few small tasks. While lying in bed after a long day of work, soccer practice with the three kids, and the heaviness of life, my husband rolled over and asked:

Business Manager: Are you going to leave me?

Me: What?

Business Manager: I don't understand why you are so unhappy. Why do you want to blog? Why do you need this? Are we not enough for you? Are you having a mid-life crisis?

I was so hurt. Why did he think I was having a mid-life crisis? Why would he think I was going to divorce him? It felt like a metric ton of poop fell onto my head at that moment in time.

I tried to reassure him that I wasn't going anywhere. I loved him. I loved the kids. I was happy with my life, but I was being pulled towards something. There was something else I was supposed to be doing. He looked scared and sad. It broke my heart to see him so vulnerable.

I kissed him and told him I would never leave. Then I rolled over and put my hand into his pants. We made love on a half inflated air mattress while trying not to wake up the kids who were in the room next to us.

The next day I sat in front of my computer and I started to think about what my husband had said the night before. Was I in the middle of a mid-life crisis? Was I going crazy? Was I selfish? Was I insane to try and chase a dream at this point in my life? So I did what I had done for the past year, I wrote. I was nervous while I was punching the keys. What would my husband think when he read this?

It's Not A Mid-Life Crisis, It's A Quest

I am thirty five years old. I have three children. I love my husband, I work full time, I take care of most of my wifely duties each day. Some days are much harder than others (wink). Some days are wonderful. I have been working on establishing a writing career for a year. It has been challenging to say the least. With my full-time job requiring constant attention, the kids, the house, the laundry, the dishes, dinner, my writing has not gotten the attention it needs to become a paying career. I love to write. I really love to write.

The past year of my life has been very interesting. I started a blog. I have performed stand-up comedy. I have been on a talk radio show. I have been featured on some big online publications. I have seen success, just not economic success. I want to one day be able to walk away from my job and launch a career that will help pay the bills, and truly feed my soul.

My marriage has struggled this year. My husband is worried that I am searching for a new life. He is concerned that I am unhappy and that I will leave. He is worried I will find a new man, and ditch him with the kids. My husband is scared. He is frustrated. He is angry. He is vulnerable. He told me he is worried that I am having a mid-life crisis. That makes me sad.

I don't want to go anywhere. I love my husband. He is my best friend. I would die for him and my children. I wouldn't trade them in for a new sports car version of a man for any amount of money or fame. He is however right, I am searching. I am reinventing myself. I am changing. I am growing. I am in the middle of a Mid-life quest for identity. My identity wasn't lost or stolen. My identity was simply hiding, waiting for the right time to show itself.

I want to obtain my dreams. I want to become the best version of me. I want to be happy in both my professional and personal life. I want to share my voice, my stories, my humor, my tale. I want him to understand that this is not about him, it's about me. This is about my identity, my story.

I have spent the past twelve years of my life devoted to my husband and the kids. I will continue to be the best wife and mother that I can be. I forget to make dinner some nights. I forget to switch the laundry (every damn time). I forget to pack lunches, but I get up and do it over and over because I love them.

My love for my family and my dream to become a writer are separate. My dreams didn't end when I got married. They didn't end when I had kids. They are inside of my heart, impatiently waiting to be realized. My quest to find my identify will be a benefit to everyone in the family. I am simply trying to be the best me that I have always wanted to be. This is not a mid-life crisis. It is a quest. It's not about him. It's about me.

This has been one of my favorite pieces to date. It brought about a ton of positive and negative comments. It also made me realize that my journey is about way more than my own quest. My journey is about a community. My journey is about giving a voice to everyone who feels the way I do, but can't express themselves for one reason or another. I think after reading this piece, my husband understood what I needed to do. It wasn't a *want*. Writing for me is a *need*. This community is a *need*. It is my passion.

Being married is a daily challenge. Marriage is not just the pretty pictures we post on Facebook, or the picture perfect Christmas cards. The real challenge is grinding through the poop that life throws at us and our spouses. The real challenge includes the hard, the messy, the "I want to hit you with my car" moments.

The real challenge is knowing that there is more to life than perfect pictures and anniversary gifts. The real challenge is knowing that the person who is sleeping next to us, snoring like a Mack truck, has our back no matter what. They are there for us even when we want to give up.

I'm not a lovie-dovie person, but I agree that love is a challenge and it needs to be cultivated and crafted every day. Without care and attention, it will grow cold and wither. The challenge continues as love grows. I'm pretty sure there is no finish line. The challenge is part of the journey.

We need to remember to thank our spouses. We need to remind them that we love them even when we want to smack them for leaving their dirty underwear *next* to the laundry basket. We need to make them a priority.

Marriage poop is difficult to scoop. It is mentally exhausting. As we grow and change so do our relationships. It was very difficult for my husband to watch me start this adventure. He did not want me taking time away from him or the family to work on my blog. Family does come first, but I needed him to understand that this was my baby. I had a fire in my belly and I needed to see this through. I needed to chase this dream. I also needed his support. I needed him to be on my team, to be my number one cheerleader.

Now, as we are approaching the second year of the blog, he is officially my Business Manager and my loudest sideline cheerleader. It was not easy for him to watch me grow and change. It was not easy for him to change his mindset. Marriage is not easy. He had to make a choice to be on my team. He has made sacrifices for me and my dream, the way I have for him and the kids. He is not only my best friend, he is my husband, and my partner; in both business and pleasure. So we scoop the marriage poop together with a very large shovel.

7. DREAM POOP

We all have dreams. We can pretend that they don't exist, but they are always there. Some of us always seem to have our heads in the clouds, while others of us run away from their dreams. I married young. I only had a vague idea of who I was at twenty three years old. I knew I loved my husband, and that was all I felt I needed to know. I wasn't sure what I wanted to be when I grew up, but I knew I loved him and that was enough for me. We did what most couples do, and we started a family. Life took over and I ran away from me. The daily grind of work, the house, and three kids took its toll. I was a wife, a mother, employee; but I was no longer myself.

That was a very scary thought. I was lost. Where had I gone? Would I be able to find myself? Was it wrong to go looking? Should I have just stayed right where I was and learned to be happy? I tried that for a few years. I tried to find fulfillment in my career, but my job was not my passion. I gave all of me to my husband and the kids, but there was still a void. I was lost. It was like the most tense, uncomfortable game of hide and seek I had ever played. I was scared that I would not like what I found if I kept looking, but I was also deathly afraid that if I stopped looking I would completely fade away into darkness. Outside of my fear of dying, this was the most crippling fear of my life. I was lost.

It was like every other thought that entered my mind was prompting me to do something. I would be at the grocery store, checking off items on my list, and the next thought was, "You are not doing what you need to do. You are wasting time." I did not want to be pondering my life's journey in the frozen food section, but that was exactly what was happening. I was holding a frozen pizza and thinking, "Why can't I figure out what I am supposed to be doing with my life? Why am I so sad? This is the wrong pizza, the kids won't eat supreme."

This voice followed me everywhere I went. It was with me the moment I woke up. It was whispering while I was doing laundry. It spoke to me in the drop off line at school. It was always there. I needed to get serious and figure this out. I needed to be honest with myself. Who was I and why was I having such a hard time figuring it out? I was still Meredith, but after years of marriage, three kids, and a career that was not feeding my soul, I was much like the Grinch's heart; cold, dead, and too many sizes too small to feel what I needed to feel.

Many of us have been here. Many of us have had these thoughts. Many of us are scared to say them out loud. We are not alone. So many of us feel this exact same way, but we are ashamed to utter the words out loud. We fear the shame that will come along with others knowing that we have dreams, knowing that we are more than wives and mothers, more than employees and house keepers. We are more than eggplant holders and grocery shoppers. The first time I said the words, "I want more" out loud was terrifying and so satisfying all at the same time. I needed more. I had to go out and find what I was missing. I was not a bad wife, a bad mother, or a bad person, for wanting more. We are told from a very young age that we are supposed to grow up, get married, have babies, and be happy. It's like our life's purpose is to make sure that everyone else is happy and in turn that will make us happy. That is true to a point. I love to make my husband and children happy, to see smiles on their faces gives me joy. I adore and love them more than anything else on this planet. Making them happy, however, is not my sole purpose on this planet. I am more than a wife, Mother, laundress, grocery shopper, and house keeper. I have dreams.

I always wanted to be on Saturday Night Live. It was my favorite television show while growing up. I loved the way the actors were able to become different characters in a matter of minutes. They would transform who they were from skit to skit. It amazed me to watch them transform. I always loved making people laugh. I always loved telling stories. I'm not going to lie, I find pleasure in making others laugh, it fills part of this void. I need it. I'm not sure why I need it, but I'd like to think that when someone laughs at my jokes, I know that for a mere second, they are happy and potentially find an escape from whatever poop they are scooping at that moment.

As a mother of three, I needed to find a way to tell my stories and make people laugh while still being able to take care of everyone and help financially support my family. I started my blog as a way to escape into my own world, but also to bring joy and laughter to others who could relate to my personal situation. I wanted other women and mothers to know that it is okay to laugh at life and to want more out of it.

In the beginning, I was unorganized and scattered to say the least. I had no idea what my mission or vision was. I basically started writing about my life and begging people to read my stories. I would email all of my friends and family and ask them to read my blog posts and give me feedback. I would hound my husband for his thoughts on my work and when he would give me his criticism, I would pout and stamp my foot. He was always supportive, but he never really seemed to get my stories. He never really seemed to understand my point of view. I finally realized that he was not my target audience, and although I needed his support, he was not who I was writing for. I was writing for myself, and I was writing for everyone out there who needed to feel normal in their own lives. I was writing to give people an escape from the mundane and to bring a smile to their faces. I was writing from a selfish place and I was finally okay with that. I needed to be selfish and follow my dreams.

I wrote for eight months without getting published on any major publications. I would write in my free time, I would write when I was supposed to be working. I would write when the kids would go to bed. I would write when I was supposed to be cooking dinner. I would post each week, sometimes three or four pieces a week, and think, "Will this be the post that goes viral, or makes it to a publication?"

That thought process was exhausting! Other writers, or starving artists like myself, know this thought process all too well. I put so much pressure on myself to become something that I once again found myself lost. How the hell did that happen? How did I figure out that I needed to find myself, only to lose myself? It was a constant battle. I would write, cry, post, write, laugh, email publishers, cry, fight with my husband, and start all over.

In May of 2015 I found myself on <u>The Huffington Post</u>. It was amazing to see my name on the front page of this publication. I had done what I set out to do. I made people laugh. I was published on a publication that millions of people read across the globe. I was happy for about a week. All of the sudden the voice was back. "What's next?" it said. Why the hell was the voice back? I had done what I had set out to do. I was officially a published writer. I hadn't made any money, but I was able to say I had been published on a major publication. The voice was back with a vengeance. I needed to keep going, and I wanted more. I was writing all the time, and luckily I had some offers coming in as a result of <u>The Huffington Post</u> piece. People were going to pay me to write for them! I couldn't believe it! I was contacted by Nestle to write a post about back to school for the Hot Pockets brand. I was so excited to show my husband that someone valued my writing, someone wanted my voice, my words, my story. I had arrived. I replied to the email and let them know that I was over the moon to write for them, and then it happened, we discussed compensation. I Googled what paid sponsorship writers were making per piece. I drafted an email to Nestle and let them know that I would write this piece for fifty dollars. I patiently waited a reply email and this is what I received.

Hi Meredith,

I am so excited that you are willing to write about our amazing product, Hot Pockets. We unfortunately do not pay for posts. We can however offer you coupons for our amazing product, or we can send you several varieties of our Hot Pockets.

Sincerely,
Nestle Corporate Hot Pockets Division.

Were they kidding me? They wanted me to write for them for free? Wait, what? They couldn't be serious. I texted a few of my blogging friends in the community and I explained what had happened with my email exchange. A few of my friends congratulated me, and other just giggled and said, "Welcome to the club." Apparently no one wants to pay you to write for them. To say I felt devalued would be a massive understatement. I wanted to be a writer, and I also wanted to be paid for it, but I wasn't there. I was still at "We will send you some Hot Pockets" status, not

"I want to pay you in US currency" status. So I replied to Nestle and I received eight packages of Hot Pockets later that week. We had several varieties to choose from. Apparently Hot Pockets now makes breakfast pockets, and my children were big fans of the Hickory Ham. They were very excited to see the freezer stocked with Hot Pockets. I guess I could be considered a paid writer at that point, but it was not my idea of a paying gig.

So I did what every writer does, I continued to write. I was published again and again in The Huffington Post. I was eventually picked up by Today.com and POPSUGAR. I did receive actual US currency from a few publications, which was nice. By January of 2016 I had been writing for sixteen months and I was burnt out. I was still unorganized. I was still a mess. I still had no vision. I had no mission. I was writing because I had stories to tell, but my focus was all over the place. I was fighting with my husband non-stop and I kept saying, "Why can't I figure this out? Why can't I make an impact? Is it worth all of this fighting and misery? I thought my dreams would be magical. I thought I would be happy. I thought I would be fulfilled. Why am I doing this?"

I needed to step back to evaluate the situation. I started writing because I wanted to tell my stories. I wanted to make people laugh. I needed to escape. I needed to follow my dreams. I realized that I wasn't sure what my dreams were, even after writing for over a year, I had no clear defined dreams. I did what I had done a lot of that year, I hid under my desk and I cried. I felt sorry for myself and I hid for a while. I stayed in my closet for about an hour and when my husband got home from work I told him that I was done. I didn't want to write anymore. It wasn't worth the time, the energy, the pain, and it really wasn't worth being paid in Hot Pockets.

I sat at my computer with tears streaming down my face and I wrote this:

Dear Readers,

It's not a secret that I have been struggling lately. I have been blogging for about sixteen months. I have gone off in various directions, including video, radio, stand-up comedy, and freelance writing. I feel like a squirrel on crack, and not like good Whitney Houston crack, rather BAD CRACK. I am tired of pondering. I am tired of complaining. I am tired of waiting for life. Life is here.

I am going to take a break from blogging. I can't say quit, because I love to write. I love to tell stories, and I love to share with all of you wonderful people. What I am going to do is take a step back. Because of my lack of direction, I am no closer towards a goal then I was sixteen months ago. If we're being honest, I am not sure what my goal is. I love to write. I love to make people laugh. I love to share real, honest, scary stories about life.

If you want to stay in touch, send me a friend request on Facebook. My name is Meredith

Masony. You can find me there, telling all of the same shenanigan type stories about my kids and life. When I write, I will post it there and here. I will be backing off of my Twitter, Pinterest, and That's Inappropriate Facebook accounts. I just need some time to be present for my family. I have put so much pressure on myself to become something, and the hilarious part is that I have no idea what that is. Talk about a masochist. I have been in a rat race with myself. FOR NO REASON.

Thank you for reading my work. I hope you find me when I come back.

Thank you,

Meredith

Just minutes after publishing this post, I had hundreds of friend requests on my personal Facebook page. I only had about 1,300 followers on my blog Facebook page, and the majority of those people followed me over to my personal page. I was amazed at how many people wanted to stay in touch with me. It was unbelievably overwhelming to see that people felt connected to me and didn't want me to leave. For the first time in months I felt relieved. It was like the stress had melted away. I started exercising again. I was able to "sort of" keep up with the house work and my job. I had made an impact. I made people laugh. I made people cry. I made a connection.

I spent the next month avoiding the voice. He had only stayed away for about a week after I decided to take a break. He crept in one night while I was fast asleep and woke me from my slumber. My eyes popped open and I heard him again. "What are you doing? We don't quit." I fired back, "I didn't quit. It wasn't working. I can't help that I wasn't good enough to get noticed. I tried". I laid there at two o'clock in the morning battling my internal demons, and I heard my son crying in the other room. I walked in and found him sobbing.

Five year old: I had a bad dream.

Me: What was it about?

Five year old: A monster was chasing me. He wanted to eat me, so I just kept running. I woke up and my legs hurt from all of the running.

I sat with him for a few minutes and held him while he fell back to sleep. I guess we all have demons. I guess our natural instinct is to run. I ran towards my dream after hiding from it for years, only to run away from it when it got tough. Fear is a very real, very scary, very funny thing. Fear can motivate us, or it can destroy us.

I went back to bed that night thinking that I was a coward. I had run. I ran when it got tough. I ran because I was weak. I ran because I didn't know what else to do. It had only been a week or so since I had taken a break, and I was back to battling with the voice. How on earth was I supposed to tell my husband that I heard him again? I had just explained to him that it was all too much and I needed a break. I didn't want to fight with him so I kept it to myself. I found myself writing in secret. I found myself making notes in my journal with ideas for books and videos. I found myself back in the arms of the monster (or potentially my savior - that part was still unclear). I knew that running wasn't going to work, but I kept it a secret from my husband that I was writing again.

I didn't publish anything for a month. It was a very short break. I sat down with my husband and told him that I couldn't keep the voice at bay and that I needed to be writing. He was furious. He began to yell, "We are in the same place we were back in October of 2014. You have made no progress. You have no idea what you want to do. You are not doing what you need to do to make any progress." I knew this was going to happen. He was right. I was still a mess. I was still unorganized. I still had no real idea what I wanted to do. He continued, "You can't spend time on this dream of yours when it interferes with our lives. You have to either get serious or be realistic. You don't know what you want, and it isn't fair to put us through this if you won't put the energy into doing it the right way!" WOW! What a slap in the face. He had verbally assaulted me with the truth. I needed to get serious and find a path. I needed to set some goals.

If I were honest with myself, I would admit that I had avoided setting goals for the past sixteen months because if there were no goals, I couldn't really fail. Goals, like the voice in my head, were scary. Goals

made this a real thing that could really fai
would make my dream more of a reality.
there crying, and I told him I was ready to set goals,
but that I needed help. I needed to figure out what I
wanted. I needed to be serious because I knew that
this was part of my soul and I couldn't run from it. I
had to scoop the goal poop and I really didn't want
to. Goal poop is unbelievably traumatic and scary.
Without goals, we have nothing. Zip. Zero. Zilch.
Goals are required to turn anything from a dream to
a reality. Dreams are amazing. Dreams are required to
get us motivated and started on our journeys, but
goals are also what get our asses moving so that we
can succeed. Goals are a requirement no matter how
scary they are. Goal poop is necessary poop.

I walked over to the couch and I sat next to him, with
the tears once again streaming down my face, and I
took out my trusty steno pad. I said, " I am ready to
set some goals. I need to turn my dreams into a reality
and I need your help. I can't do this alone. I need
you." He had a look of unbelief on his face but he
scooted over and let me sit next to him. He once
again asked me what my mission was. I hated the
word mission. It sounded so ridiculous. I wasn't a
soldier. I didn't have a mission. "Write down your
mission. You need a mission." So I sat on the couch,
in the spot where the dog had once peed and I began
to write what I wanted.

My Mission

I am a Mom. I had babies, not a lobotomy. I am here to tell stories about my life, my family, my struggles, and my joy. I try to find the humor in all things. I am on a quest to obtain my dreams. I want to become the best version of me. I want to be happy in both my professional and personal life. I want to share my voice, my stories, my humor, my tale.

That's Inappropriate is a platform to unify parents while we do the hardest job on the planet. Parenting is exhausting, gritty, raw, and overall joyful.

As parents, we need to make choices that affect the lives of so many other people. By injecting humor into the relatable daily struggles that we face, we can find the common ground in life's toughest job.

My mission was to unify people. My mission was to bring laughter to the hardest topics we face as parents and as people. I wanted to help people scoop their poop and find a laugh while they are eyeball deep in doo doo.

I don't think my husband was completely satisfied with this mission, but he knew I was serious about getting real and setting goals. We sat on the couch for a while talking about what I wanted to come out of this. What I really wanted to do with my voice, with my words. I knew a book was in my future, but I wasn't ready at that point, so I started with video. I explained that I wanted to start shooting videos and adding those into the blog.

I wanted to make sure that my page was a safe place where people could come and have a laugh, but also feel heard. I wanted my blog to be a place where they felt welcomed and knew that they were not alone. I had felt alone for so long and I hated the way that made me feel. I wanted to make sure that the myths about parenting being the most beautiful, easy, natural experience were debunked. Parenting can often be the most frustrating and exhausting task on the planet, and it is okay to talk about it. I wanted to make sure that people had a safe place to talk about the toughest job that we do as human beings. My mission was rooted in community. My mission was way less about me, and way more about bringing people together to support them in their daily lives as we all struggle with our parenting, our jobs, life, and scooping the poop.

8. FAMILY POOP

I always remember wanting to be a Mom. Even when I was a child, I liked to take care of other people. When I was twelve years old, my parents gave me a little sister, who I claimed as my own. She was an adorable chunky blonde baby with blue eyes. We called her "Moosearella." Her crib was in my room. I would help with feedings, and I would push her around in her stroller. We were always together, all day every day. I loved taking care of her. We were inseparable. A few years later, my parents finished the family when they had my baby brother. By the time I was sixteen, I had two car seats in my car, and I was helping with drop offs and pick-ups at daycare because my parents worked a lot.

I will never forget an interaction I had in a grocery store when I was around seventeen years old. I was picking up a few items. The normal things, like milk, bread, cheese, eggs, diapers. I had my brother on my hip, my sister was in the cart. I opened my purse to pull out some cash to pay for the groceries. As I handed the cashier the money she looked and me and said, "It is a crying shame that you have gotten yourself into this mess." I was confused as to what mess she was referring to. I said, "I'm sorry, what?" She said, "Having two children at your age, what a disgrace." I'm pretty sure I turned as white as a sheet. I put the groceries into the cart and said, "This is my brother and my sister." I pushed the cart out to the parking lot and strapped the kids into their car seats.

This interaction taught me at a very young age that perspective is very important. People have no clue what it really going on in anyone's lives, but they will take a guess and make a judgement. I bet that cashier didn't believe me. I bet she thought I was a teen Mom who continued to make poor choices in her life. The reality is, it doesn't matter. That is her poop. Not mine.

I have three siblings. I have a brother who is a year older than me. I have a sister who is twelve years younger, and a brother who is fifteen years younger. When they were older, I remember going out and having people ask us if we had different parents (which is better than assuming they were mine). Most people thought that My Mom had remarried and had two children with her new husband. I always replied, "No, my parents are just crazy." This huge age gap between me and my younger siblings has caused some friction. It has also caused me to play the role of a parent rather than a sibling.

When my sister was thirteen, I made her and her best friend come to my house to watch a movie that talked about AIDS. The movie was called, "Girl Positive." It was a lifetime movie about teenagers having unprotected sex and getting a sexually transmitted disease.

I thought my sister was going to die when I sat her and her friend down and explained that she could get AIDS from having unprotected sex. I was mortified, she was mortified, but I needed to explain this to her. I needed to know that she was going to be smart and make good choices. I needed to know that I made every effort to explain the pitfalls of dating and sex, and I wanted it to come from me. It was beyond awkward, but being a "90210" fan, it helped having Jennie Garth in my corner. Yeah, that's right. I picked a movie about sex ed. starring Kelly from "Beverly Hills 90210". Can you say "WINNING!"?

I needed to scoop that poop. I needed to take the initiative and discuss that uncomfortable situation with her. It was as much for me as it was for her. I had to own that poop. So I sat saying things like, penis, vagina, herpes, AIDS, condoms, birth control, choices, and I did it without crying. I owned that poop. It was important poop. I am proud to say that my "Birds and the Bees" conversation from 2009 was successful. My sister is a productive member of society who claims she may never want to have children. I think having a front row seat to my life may have permanently cured her from parenting.

Now that my sister is twenty five years old and grown, living in a very faraway place, I no longer need to scoop this type of poop for her. When she calls for advice, I give her my opinion, but I don't expect her to take it. She is an adult, and she can scoop her own poop. I never lie to her, but I know that as an adult she is going to do what she wants to do. I can't control her actions, and I don't want to make her choices for her. We are very different people and what makes me happy will not give her joy. It was very hard to find this place. I wanted to help her live her life, but I realized that only pushed her further away from me. So I stopped scooping her poop and I handed her the shovel. She is old enough and smart enough to scoop her own. I did all that I could. She is a good egg.

My baby brother on the other hand, Bubba, was a tough egg. When he was fifteen, I remember getting a call from the principal's office. They explained that my brother was going to be suspended from school and that I needed to go pick him up. I should have stopped the conversation right there, but of course I asked what he had done. The Dean told me how my brother had pretended to urinate in his pants because the teacher had refused to let him go to the bathroom. Apparently he had asked to go to the bathroom several times and she told him no because he was a "frequent flyer", meaning he would skip class often. He apparently wasn't going to take no for an answer so he went back to his seat and poured a water bottle on his pants and told the teacher he had "peed" himself because she wouldn't let him go. She of course panicked and told him to go to the bathroom .

After he left, she called the front office and they brought him down to discuss what happened. He told them what he had done, and ended up with a three day suspension. This was not his first time in the

Principal's office. My parents, who were called first, were done. They had been called into a meeting the week prior to discuss his grades and lack of effort. My father told the guidance counselor that, "He will be sixteen soon and can drop out. He can become a garbage man, or trade worker." The guidance counselor looked as though she had seen a ghost when my father suggested he drop out. My parents both graduated high school, but do not believe that everyone needed to finish school, or go to college for that matter. When I spoke to my Dad later that evening he told me, "We need garbage men. They make good money. He obviously doesn't want to be in school. I am not dealing with this anymore."

I took my brother home with me and sat him down at the kitchen table with my husband. "What are you doing? Why are you acting like this? Don't you care about school? Do you want to be a garbage man?" I shouted at him. He looked at me forming his teenage face into an awful scowl. I could tell he was filled with angst; angst that I didn't particularly care about. I went to high school. I graduated. I did what I needed to do, and so would he. I spoke with my parents and called a meeting at the school. My husband and I became his educational guardian and he moved in with us.

I switched him to another high school and I sat on top of him like a hawk. We did everything we could to get him on track. His grades improved. He was doing well on the baseball team. He wasn't a bad kid, be just need someone to help him scoop his poop. My husband and I needed to do that. It wasn't easy. I had to go to the high school a few times and show up for surprise inspections. One time I got a call from his history teacher that he had missed a few classes. I called to make sure that he was in school one morning and I drove over, got my visitor pass, and walked into his classroom. I opened the door and asked him if he needed help finding his history class. He said no, but I explained that I had gotten a call letting me know that he had not been in that class twice this week. I asked him to come into the hallway with me to discuss the situation. As he got up I grabbed him by the arm and took off my flip flop. I smacked him on the backside as he walked out of the class while twenty five of his classmates watched him receive his flip flop beating.

He needed me to be the one who scooped his poop. He needed me to smack him with a flip flop. When he graduated from high school I wept like a baby. I was so proud that he stuck it out. He didn't go to college, but he is doing great, working a trade and making more money than I am, and he is only twenty one years old. He has already purchased a home and he is one hundred percent self-sufficient. He has his own shovel now, and he is doing a fantastic job scooping his own poop. He still calls and asks for advice, but like my sister, I tell him what I think and I do not expect him to take my advice. He has his poop together. He doesn't need me to be his scooper anymore.

I love my siblings. We are all very different people. My oldest brother has four kids of his own. He has a wonderful wife and they are fantastic parents. My sister is growing up and chasing her dream right out of the gate. She amazes me every day. She has no fear. My Bubba will be successful, no doubt in my mind. He is a fighter and even if he fails, he will get back up and push through. I am proud of all of them. I will always be there for them if they need help scooping. It was tough to realize that they don't need me to scoop for them any longer. It was like a weird "empty nest" situation when I realized I no longer needed to help them scoop their poop. It was also a relief. They've got this.

Many of us have siblings that are constantly requiring that we scoop their poop. Consider: Who is it benefiting? We may feel good by helping them, we may even feel obligated to do it, but what it is really doing for them? When we scoop someone's poop for too long, we become enablers. If we enable our siblings, they will never learn to scoop for themselves.

My parents, thankfully, were not enablers because they were very young when they had me. My Mom was nineteen when she had my brother and twenty when she had me. They were fresh out of high school and still kids themselves. I grew up in a home with a lot of yelling and fighting. The stress of having young children while working pay check to pay check jobs was hard on everyone.

I love my parents, but growing up I feared my Father and often times ignored my Mother. Growing up in a household of four children and being occasionally responsible for the two younger siblings was rather challenging. I had changed more diapers by the time I was fifteen, then most first time parents did in year one.

We were not a hugging family. We didn't shout "I love you" across the room. We weren't sentimental or overly emotional. That does not mean we didn't love each other or look out for one another. It did cause me to have some major personal space issues, I would rather shake hands than hug, but I am working on that. I do hug my children, and relatives get one birthday hug a year, I'm not the Grinch.

My parents taught me the importance of working hard. Nothing worthwhile in life will ever be handed to me. We all have to work hard. We have to be patient. We have to be dedicated. I have no doubt that work ethic is a learned behavior. Both my Mom and Dad are extremely hard working people. I'd like to think I am a hard worker. I know that I am a dreamer, but the past two years of my life I have worked to turn my dream into a reality. I have spent weekends, holidays, days off, and burned plenty of midnight oil to turn this dream into a reality. Hard work requires sacrifice.

My parents inadvertently taught me how important it is to tell my children how I feel about them. I don't remember my parents telling me they were proud of me or that they loved me. I knew they did. It was simply implied. But as an adult, I can tell you, that I needed to actually hear those words when I was younger. I spent most of my life searching for approval and love. I needed to know that I was special. I needed to know that I mattered.

Now that I am a parent, I tell my kids as often as I can that I love them and I am proud of them. I don't care if they are athletes, band geeks, karate ninjas, or chess players. I am simply proud of my kids for pooping and wiping their butts. That is a massive achievement. With my youngest in kindergarten, I am new to the "Non-butt wiping club." I gotta say I love it here. I am proud that my children are self-sufficient butt wipers. We still have lightning streaked undies on occasion, but we are close. I don't want my children to search for approval. I want them to always go to bed knowing that they are loved and that they are enough. I don't want my children to have to scoop the emotional poop I grew up with. It took me years to let that poop go. It took my years to realize that I was enough.

I have realized that I cannot scoop my parent's poop. I wish they would spend more time with my children. I wish they would call me more often to see how things are going. I don't reach out as often as I should because I don't want to fight with them or explain why I blog about underwear. I no longer search for their approval. Their approval won't give me anything I can't get on my own.

I know that my Father and his Mother had a very rough relationship. I know that it caused my Dad to raise us the way he did. That is his poop. I can't scoop it for him. If he wants to have a better relationship with me, he will need to address that. I can't feel badly about our relationship because I can't change how he views his poop. I can just love him the way he is and know that he loves me the best way he can.

Parent poop runs deep. We all have it. My Mom and Dad taught me the lessons I needed to be the best sibling, parent, and wife I can be. I love them and I am grateful they are my parents. As we get older we learn how important family is. My parents may not always agree with the choices I make, but I know that they love me.

We do not get to pick our parents. We certainly don't get to pick our second set of parents- the in-laws. Most of us marry the man, not the second mom and dad. But when we get married, we have to shovel an enormous amount of in-law poop.

Let me broach this subject with the fact that I do indeed love my In-Laws, but sometimes they drive me crazy. They are fantastic grandparents and I know that they would do anything for us, but sometimes I hit the ignore button rather than answer the phone when my Mother in law calls. I'm pretty sure she does the same thing to me.

My husband and I have been married for fourteen years. He is Puerto Rican and I am as white bread as they come. My husband was not raised in the same kind of household as I was. There was no lack of hugging, and plenty of "I love yous" were flying around. He was raised on a small island off of Puerto Rico by a very large, very loud family.

My husband is also the baby of the family, and I am positive that his Mother was not too pleased with our relationship. I am sure I will feel the same way she did when I am getting ready to marry off my sons. I can hear myself now, "What is he thinking, dating that trollop." Hopefully I will learn from my relationship with my MIL and not go down that road.

After we had children, it was hard for my MIL to understand that *her* rules were not *our* rules. We were the parents, which meant she did not always get her way. I remember sitting on the phone with her, listening to her tell me why I was parenting wrong and I could feel my blood boiling to the surface. I hung up the phone and screamed at my husband. "What is wrong with your Mother? Why does she treat me like I don't know how to raise my children?" He fired back with, "At least my parents care. At least they help with the kids." At the end of that interaction, we were both upset and both hurt by what the other had said. It took me years to realize that I can't fix my MIL's poop, and her poop really has nothing to do with me.

My MIL is welcome to her opinion, because it really doesn't affect me. She is welcome to think, believe, and feel however she wants. I don't need to change that. In fact, I need to respect that. Everyone is entitled to an opinion, that doesn't make their opinion accurate or truthful, it simply makes it "Theirs."

Last year before school started I was talking with her about backpacks. I told her I was going to buy them later in the week when I had a chance to go out. I had talked with the kids and they had each requested various superhero character backpacks. Two days later, my MIL shows up at the door with brand new back packs, and the kids were overjoyed. Just as I was about to get upset because I specifically told her I was going to get backpacks, I was relieved. She had saved me a trip to the store and about $40! This was a win. I didn't have to look at this as an attack on me. She wanted to buy the backpacks and now I had one less thing to do, and extra money for Starbucks in my pocket. Five years ago, that interaction would have thrown me over the edge. Today I look at that poop and I have learned that I don't need to scoop that poop.

We had a bumpy start, but time and again my in-laws have shown me that they will go above and beyond for my family. What I deem as intrusive, they deem as helpful. I have learned to talk about the issues we face and be honest with how it makes me feel. I have also learned that I need to stop trying to change them. If I want something to change, I need to figure out how to be that change. I need to worry about scooping my own poop long before I scoop in-law poop. By understanding that I can only control my actions and reactions I am happier and less stressed. I enjoy our time more and I am more respectful of their feelings. They just want to spend time with us and the kids. They want to be a part of our lives.

Unfortunately, not everyone is as lucky as I am. Other people suffer from toxic in-law poop, and should take a step back and think about where their in-laws are coming from. Is it a place of love? If not, they may need to be removed from the family's life. If they are hurtful or destructive, it is not our jobs to fix them.

We can't scoop their poop.

For those of us with in-laws like mine, who are legitimately coming from a place of love, we should be the change we want to see in the relationship. I guarantee that they will be receptive to positive loving behavior. It is never easy to take the first step. We all want the other person to be the one who offers the olive branch. If we each bite the bullet and extend the peace, we will all reap the benefits. We need to scoop our poop first. It is the only poop we have any control over

9. MY POOP

We all have poop. We have past poop, which we cannot change. We have current poop, which is what we are physically dealing with right this minute in our lives. And, we have future poop. Future poop can be very difficult to deal with. We spend a ton of time worrying about future poop, which is odd because we have very little, if any control over future poop.

Let's take a look at past poop. Like everyone else on this planet, I have past poop. I spent a lot of time battling my past poop. I spent a lot of time trying to find validation because I didn't get that during my childhood. I needed to know that I was "Good enough."

About a year ago while at church one Sunday, the topic of the sermon was self-worth. The pastor went into great detail about how humans determine their self-worth. I sat still and quiet as I listened to him ask the following questions:

"What did you see the last time you looked in a mirror? Did you see black bags under your eyes? A receding hairline? Perhaps you saw a body you love, or one that causes you

anxiety and shame. Did you see someone who has it all together, or someone who is holding on by a thread? How do we determine what we are worth?"

I have had some issues with what my worth is lately. I have been working on my writing career, while "busting hump", as my father would say with my full-time job. I have three kids, two dogs, and one husband to look after. I would say my worth is a composite of many factors. The problem for many of us is that we see and hear what others are telling us and we judge our worth based on others' opinions as well as lies created by our subconscious.

Take a look at these five factors that were outlined in the pastor's sermon that people use to determine their worth.

Five Factors For Determining Self-Worth and my Response

1. **Financial success:** Most people judge their worth based on how much money they make. If I base my burgeoning writing career on my current financial status, I am a failure. I have been paid in Hot Pockets, Fruit of the Loom underwear, and a total of $350 over the past fourteen months. Breaking that down, I have made less than a dollar a day. I am not even going to count how much I have spent on my burgeoning writing career. I have, however, gone from zero views on my website in October of 2014 to over 650,000 in October of 2016.

2. **Physical Appearance:** I have more gray hair, wrinkles, upper lip hair, sagging skin, and gravitationaly challenged breasts than I had last year. I can look in the mirror and find at least 100 flaws. I can also look in the mirror and see that I am alive despite a third surgery this year. My wrinkle lines are a prize of hard work and determination, and the breasts, well I have absolutely no control over those. They did feed three children.

3. **Facebook Status:** I have a mild Facebook addiction. I scroll through my feed looking into the lives of friends and family. I see their smiles, new cars, fancy dresses, new houses, and nausea inducing messages to their spouses. I see the perfect picture, like a Thomas Kinkaid landscape, simple perfection. It is hard to remember that what I see is not the whole picture. These updates are just what people want us to see. It can be so depressing to see how much better others seem to be doing. But please, don't judge Facebook by its cover. We are all hiding something. People don't want us to know that they silently suffer with hemorrhoids, that their kid was suspended from school last week, or that they hate their in-laws. We post what we want others to believe is our reality. The reason I post about every aspect of my life is simply because I don't want other moms to suffer with hemorrhoids in silence. I want everyone to have a hemorrhoid partner in crime.

4. **Families:** With life going by at a million miles a minute, it is hard to remember that my kids are just that, kids. They throw temper tantrums in public at times. They need constant attention that leaves me physically and emotionally drained at times. They make poor choices and tap dance on my last nerve like someone is paying them good money to do it. They also bring me more joy than anything else on this planet. Two out of three of my children can read now. All of my children love me right where I am in my journey.

5. **Marriage:** My marriage has had quite a ride this year - major ups and downs. We have had conversations that made my head explode. I have gone to bed quietly crying so my husband couldn't hear me. I have also learned more about him in this past year than I have in the past twenty years. We have grown closer as a couple. We have become better spouses to each other. We have become better parents together.

If determining my worth is based on a composite score of the above five topics, I am doing pretty great. The problem is that I am my biggest critic. I give myself undesirable ratings in these categories on a daily basis. I need to learn to lighten up and give myself a fair shake. I advise everyone to do the same. We should all take a look at these aspects of our lives. We should compare where we are from last year to today. Have we changed? Have we grown? Have we learned anything over the past year? My guess is yes. My guess is that we are all worth way more than we give ourselves credit for. My guess is that we are doing so much more "right" than we are "wrong". We all have worth. We can't rob ourselves of the value that we have cultivated over our lifetimes. We need to celebrate our accomplishments and enjoy the gifts we bring to the table. We are worth more than we will ever know.

It took me thirty five years to finally figure out that I was the one who was able to determine that I was in fact "Good enough." I was the only one who was able to determine if I had put in enough effort. I was the only one who knew if I gave my all. I was the one who could determine my value. No one else could set a value for me. I had to figure out how to let go of my past poop. I am not a therapist, but what I do know is that my past helped create who I currently am. If I am happy with where I am in my life, I need to be okay with my past.

So where does that leave me? It leaves me scooping my current poop and rejecting the shame that others try to impose on me.

As a mother, wife, employee, daughter, daughter in law, friend, and human being, I feel as though sometimes people try to shame me into doing things, feeling things, explaining things, etc. I am here to say that I reject being shamed. Below is a list of things I do, and that I refuse to feel guilty for.

I refuse to feel guilt for the following things: (These are in no specific order.)

1. Forgetting to cook dinner. (2X a week.)

2. Forgetting to switch the laundry for the 37th time. (Every. Damn. Day.)

3. Forgetting it's picture day at my kids school. (3 kids, 3 schools. It's gonna happen.)

4. Hitting up the drive-thru after a three hour soccer practice. (Once a week.)

5. Missing soccer practice. (Sometimes. They aren't on the USA Olympic team.)

6. Missing dance practice. (Sometimes. She isn't in the Russian ballet house.)

7. Forgetting to sign my kids' agendas. It's first grade, not Harvard. (Happens 2X a week.)

8. Not paying the water bill, light bill, car payment, credit card bill. (I forget. They always call.)

9. Missing a workout at the gym.(At least one a week.)

10. Flossing my kids' teeth. Baby teeth do fall out, right? (I hand them the floss, what they do with it is a mystery.)

11. Not picking up the toy room before I go to bed. (I start to clean up, but sometimes I get side tracked.)

12. Not throwing out the coffee grinds after I finish the pot of coffee. (Every. Damn. Time.)

13. Missing trash day. (Once a week.)

14. Forgetting the mail for three days in a row. (Every three days.)

15. Being the last parent at daycare pick up. (2X a week.)

16. Being late. (Every. Damn. Time.)

17. Being moody. (While actively parenting or at work.)

18. Being loud. (My husband says deaf people can hear me.)

19. Being drunk. (Not while actively parenting or at work.)

20. Being annoyed. (See #17.)

21. Being honest. (I'm always honest.)

22. Being sarcastic. (I'm always sarcastic. I don't know any other language.)

23. Dropping my kids off at school in my yoga pants. (I like yoga pants.)

24. Picking my kids up from school in my yoga pants. (See #23.)

25. Not brushing my hair. I usually always brush my teeth. (Usually.)

26. Wearing a "#MOMosa" hat pretty much every day of my life. (I like my hat.)

27. Burning dinner. I know I have a timer on the microwave, but I am doing fifty things while cooking dinner, and I wouldn't hear the damn thing beep anyway. (I burn everything.)

28. Forgetting to iron. (Once a week.)

29. Misplacing my keys. (3X a week.)

30. Misplacing my phone. (6X a day.)

31. Misplacing my shoes. (2X a day.)

32. Forgetting to pack lunches. (2X a week.)

33. Forgetting to get an oil change. (I am not positive my car actually needs oil. Could be a conspiracy.)

34. Forgetting to get gas. (Yes, I have a gas light, but I forget that I saw it and I drive home.)

35. Not being able to help my first grader with her math homework. (I married someone who can do math.)

36. Not being able to help my fourth grader with his math homework. (See #35.)

37. Forgetting to return something someone let me borrow. Once I borrow it, I will forget you lent it to me and never give it back. (Every single time I borrow something. No exceptions.)

38. Forgetting a birthday (Happens a ton.)

39. Forgetting an anniversary. (I honestly only remember my anniversary.)

40. Forgetting an appointment. (I do this a ton.)

41. The way my children act in public. They know better, but they are kids, and sometimes they forget. I promise I will remind them when we are not in public. (I have lots of flip flops.)

42. Being too tired to bake Pinterest inspired cupcakes for my kids birthdays. My Publix has cake making on lock. (I can't bake no-bake items.)

43. Anything else that I missed that someone else feels I should be doing, but I am currently not doing. (I am out of shits to give.)

I do my very best every single day. I give 100%, 100% of the time. I am one person. I try to do several things all at once. I am no June Cleaver, but I am also not Mrs. Bates from Psycho. I find that I fall somewhere between Peg Bundy and Claire Dunphy.

I try to find humor in all things, because it is much easier to laugh off the life-poop. Most days I survive and get most things done. It is fine to survive the current poop. We have to do that. We have to scoop each day so we can get up and do it all over again.

Sometimes nothing goes right. Sometimes I get scared at how awesome things are going. One thing I am positive of is that I am at a point in my life where I reject being shamed. I wish that all of the "Shamers" out there would think about the shoes that other people walk in. Life needs to be celebrated. If all of the members in my household are safe, fed, and put to bed, I am going to raise a glass of wine to a successful day.

Being okay with my past has given me a better perspective on the current poop that I deal with. The daily grind poop can be overwhelming, but it requires constant scooping. Every day of my life I wake up and think hundreds of thousands of thoughts. I think all day long, every damn day. Even when I sleep, I have constant lists and topics running wild through my cerebellum. It. Is. Exhausting. I love my husband. I love my kids. However, I would love to sleep. The mythological creature known as "Sleep" has eluded me for quite some time now. I am positive that I am the one who robs myself of sleep. My mind, like my home, is never quiet. I use to wish for quiet. If you are like me, you have had several if not all of these thoughts.

1. Is that a foot in my face?

2. Why does my hair smell like pee?

3. What day is it?

4. Did I pack lunches last night?

5. Where is the toilet paper? I know I bought toilet paper. Why isn't it in this cabinet? I just went to the grocery store. Oh wait, that was last week. Not this week. Maybe I didn't buy toilet paper.

6. I have to get everyone up and ready. But it is so quiet. I just want them to sleep until lunch.

7. Okay, get them up. Push the coffee pot button first. At least the smell of coffee will soothe me.

8. Why are they fighting already? They haven't been up for five freaking minutes. How can anyone be this angry all the time?

9. Why does everyone ask me where everything is? I can't remember where I put *my* shoes, let alone *your* shoes.

10. It isn't even eight o'clock in the morning yet. Dear sweet Lord help me!

11. We can make it to school on time if we leave right now.

12. We will only be five minutes late if we leave right now.

13. Where are my keys?

14. How on earth have they not brushed their teeth yet? I don't care if he is the smelly kid in class. Just go to the car.

15. Okay, relax. I can feel my blood pressure skyrocketing.

16. Oh, I like this song. Why do I like this song. There are only five total words in this song. I used to be smart.

17. Okay, 2 kids dropped off. One more to go.

18. Okay, off to work. Why am I sweating

already? I think I smell.

19. Don't forget to switch the laundry when I get home. It may be moldy. I forgot to switch it last night.

20. Take something out for dinner. What did we have yesterday? How do I not remember what I made yesterday?

21. Spaghetti. We had spaghetti! I knew I would remember. Well I guess we can't have spaghetti.

22. What time is it?

23. Why are these leftovers in the fridge? I told him to take this as his lunch. How does he forget his lunch every freaking day? I should call and see if he needs lunch.

24. I better vacuum. What is that spot on the floor? Why is it sticky? We didn't have pancakes today. Is that maple syrup?

25. Okay, two hours until pick up. What do I need to do? Shit! I forgot to switch the laundry.

26. Okay, I need to wash this again.

27. Off to pick up. I will switch this when I get home.

28. Did I forget to turn the crock pot on? I didn't smell food.

29. Okay. Two kids picked up, one to go.

30. Why are they fighting? They just got in the car. Why do they hate me?

31. Shit! I forgot to turn the crock pot on. Okay, that will be dinner tomorrow. We can do breakfast for dinner tonight.

32. One hour until they go to bed. I can do this. Sixty minutes.

33. Who threw that ball at my head? Freaking kids! Seriously. They hate me.

34. Forty minutes until bed. I can do this.

35. They just need to shower and brush teeth. Maybe tonight will be the night they do it all by themselves.

36. Why do I have to help them every night? We brush teeth every night. It is not rocket science.

37. Ten minutes. I can do this.

38. Seriously kid, go to bed. If they come out and ask for water one more time.

39. Okay, it is quiet. I am so happy to be sitting down right now.

40. I am so tired. I can't see straight.

41. Did he just ask me if I want to do it? Seriously? Is he insane?

42. Is he seriously pouting right now?

43. It will only take five minutes, just suck it up and do it so he will go to bed.

44. Okay, I can go to bed in ten minutes and I will get a solid six hours of sleep.

45. Okay, brain shut off. It is bedtime.

46. What was that noise? Is a kid awake?

47. I better check on the kids.

48. Okay, everyone is fine.

49. I am so tired!

50. Shit! I forgot to switch the laundry.

There is no off switch. We just keep moving forward like the Energizer bunny on crack. Day in, day out. I am positive there are times when we all feel this way. We all deserve a round of applause for our efforts to make it from sunrise to sunset while we scoop the poop.

It took me thirty five years to let go of the past and realize that I am just fine. I am enough. I am strong. My current poop is like most everyone else's poop. It is the daily grind poop. It is the kid poop. It is the marriage poop. What I chose to do with my current poop is express it so that it doesn'tc build up. That sounds pretty awful, what I mean is that I write and shoot video about my current poop so that other people can relate to it and find some peace with their own poop. We should own our poop! We should love our poop! We can scoop our poop!

Back when I wrote "It's Not A Crisis It's A Quest" I had hundreds of people contact me to tell me that they loved and hated the piece. That told me a few very important things. It told me that my words resonated with people, and that they also struck a nerve. I wrote about my quest because I wanted to uncover the way I was feeling and I wanted to let other women know that it was okay to have these thoughts and feelings. It was normal to want more. The response I received told me that I am not alone. There are many women out there who are feeling the same way I am. There are many women who are trying to balance the craziness of life while remaining true to themselves.

The other thing this post taught me, is that people are angered and vehemently opposed to change and growth. The piece is about self-exploration and a quest for meaning. The post is about knowing who I am and being comfortable in my skin. The piece is about the journey I was, and still am, undertaking.

The stereotypical mid-life crisis of the 1970's may still exist, but that is not my crisis. I am not sure if I am choosing to have a different crisis, or if women just so happen to have a different type of crisis. My crisis shall furthermore be called a quest. My crisis shall be an educational journey into my mind and soul. My crisis will result in the betterment of myself and my family. Why? Because I get to choose how I live and deal with my crisis.

Women are perceptive, emotional, conceptual, intelligent, motivated beings. We can quest for whatever the hell we want to quest for, even if our quest requires industrial-strength shovels.

10 Things This Quest Is NOT About:

1. This is not about replacing my husband and family.

2. This is not about becoming a new person.

3. This is not about running away.

4. This is not about complaining and being unhappy.

5. This is not about judgment and throwing stones at my husband.

6. This is not about having an affair to fill an emotional void.

7. This is not about being less of a Mom or shrugging my responsibilities.

8. This is not about choosing to let my children suffer to make myself happy.

9. This is not about marrying young and not knowing who I am.

10. This is not about YOU!

10 Things This Quest IS ABOUT:

1. This is about discovering my talents and passions.

2. This is about allowing myself to be the person I was meant to be.

3. This is about running towards my goals and dreams.

4. This is about finding balance.

5. This is about finding a way to bring my family with me on my quest.

6. This is about learning to fill the void by giving myself permission to quest for my passion.

7. This is about having no regrets.

8. This is about paving the way for other women to find their voice.

9. This is about using my voice to tell MY story.

10. This is about MY quest, MY family's role in the quest, and MY determination for it to be a success.

When we feel this way, we should stop what we are doing and evaluate. We need to evaluate our lives, our relationships, our goals, and our dreams. We need to evaluate our POOP. We cannot stay complacent so that we avoid rocking the boat. Regrets will sink a ship faster than an iceberg. It won't be easy, but I guarantee that it will be worth it.

Once we put regrets behind us, it is a bit easier to begin focusing on our future poop. Future poop is unbelievably scary though. I ask myself, "Will I eventually become a success? Will I ever make any money? Will I be able to feel satisfaction? Will the voice ever stop?" Future poop haunts my daydreams and my nightmares. We all have future poop. Will the kids be successful? Will my husband stay with me if I chase my dreams? Will my anyone buy my book?

Future poop is the hardest for me to scoop. I know that I have no control over what will happen next. Future poop can be daunting. So just like any other kind of poop, I scoop it as it comes my way. I try to remember to breathe and take it in stride, but it is never easy. The "what ifs" are the hardest to digest.

When I was pregnant with my first child I was placed on bed rest and every day I worried that he was going to be born prematurely. I worried about his health. I worried that I would never get to be a Mom. My grandmother came to the hospital to see me after I went into pre-term labor at twenty four weeks. I was crying and said, "What if he dies?" She took my hand and said, "Right now he is not your baby. He is God's baby. Right now all you can do is sit here and do what the doctors tell you to do. You are already his Mother, but God will give you a son when he is ready. This is not in your control. This is not for you to worry about."

How was I supposed to not worry. How was I supposed to sit and wait and be patient? I sat there and cried. It was the longest fourteen weeks of my life, but my grandmother was right. I could only do what the doctors told me to do. I had no control. The future is a very scary place. I may write this book and not sell a single copy. I might never make back the investment I have made on my blog, my videos, my book, or my camera and computer equipment. I may never become a sitcom writer, or take my book on tour. The only thing I can currently control is the energy and effort that I put into my projects. I can only control certain tiny aspects of this adventure. I do know that my adventure has not been in vain. I have brought joy to people and to myself. I have provided an escape from daily life. I have found a way to find my people and discuss the dirty messy topics that relate to daily life and parenting. No one can take away what I have already created with my heart, sweat, and tears. It is mine. The future cannot rob me of my current status. Only I can rob me of that.

10. HATER POOP

We all have haters. In my world on social media, my haters are people I don't know, and they try to rob me of my joy on a daily basis. My haters are people who troll my social media accounts and leave me awful, hateful messages. Haters can be anyone. They can be family, frenemies, even employers. What do we do when we are confronted with hater poop?

I have been pretty lucky with my family. I do have family members who do not like that I blog, or the topics that I discuss, but they don't publically bash me. For the most part, my family is supportive of my journey and they want me to succeed. Others of us are not this lucky and have family haters. These people need to make sure to set boundaries. Opinions are fine, but if someone has a family member who is blasting them for chasing their dreams, the way they raise their children, or their marriage, then they should be firm with their boundaries. If someone is spreading hate about us, then that means we have struck a nerve with them and they feel insecure in their own lives.

It is easy to say sticks and stones may break my bones, but names will never hurt me. It was much harder to be told I was a worthless piece of shit who is an alcoholic parent, and the reason our society is so awful. When on social media, it doesn't take long to start receiving hateful comments. I have been told that I am ugly, that I am an awful parent, that my children should be placed with child protective services because I am abusive. I have been told by strangers that my husband obviously cheats on me because I am an awful wife, and that I obviously cheat on him because I am chasing a dream instead of being the wife and mother that my family needs. Strangers have violated me and my family more times than I would like to discuss, but that's okay. I am not what the haters say I am. One of my favorite comments to date came back in March of 2016. Check out what Cliff had to say about me:

> "Look at this transvestite looking "women", talking about penis size when "her' nose is the size of a toucan parrot and her teeth look like plank boards painted white! Not to mention the self-absorbed, grating voice that "she's" obviously not aware of!□ "

I had a few thoughts when I read this comment. First, how does he know if a parrot is a transvestite? Second, I wanted to thank him. I do spend a lot of time on my dental hygiene. I make sure to brush at least two to three times a day, and despite recent research against flossing, I floss regularly. My final thought was, is my voice really that awful? My kids do complain about my singing voice, but I had no idea my voice was self-absorbed.

I had a bit of fun with Cliff and we went back and forth:

> *Cliff*: Look at this transvestite looking "women", talking about penis size when "her" nose is the size of a toucan parrot and her teeth look like plank boards painted white! Not to mention the self-absorbed, grating voice that "she's" obviously not aware of!☐

> *That's Inappropriate*: Thanks for the morning pep talk. Have a great day.☐

> *Cliff*: No problem! ...and hey, don't nick your chin shaving this morning!☐

> *That's Inappropriate*: Awesome tip. I'll keep that in mind.☐

> *Cliff*: That a boy!☐

> *That's Inappropriate:* I also appreciated the compliment about how white my teeth are. I am vigilant about my brushing.☐

It is always best to avoid contact with internet trolls, but I did have fun with Cliff. His opinion of me and my parrot like features have no impact on who I am. I am, in fact, NOT a transvestite parrot. His words, although on the internet forever, did not become truth. His hate can hurt my feelings, but only if I allowed them to. Cliff couldn't break me if I didn't allow him to.

I could fill an entire book with the hate that people send my way. I don't want to spend tons of time on the negativity. I do want to state that we can find the positive side of everything, including hater poop. There is in fact a silver lining to hater poop. I do like Taylor Swift has instructed and I shake it off. I get up and I keep going. I use the hater poop to push forward and spread my voice, my stories, my tales.

If I had a nickel every time I uttered the words "I can't" I would be a millionaire for sure. We all say these words, almost every day, even without the haters probing us. Why do we do it? Why is it that we think we can't do something? When I first started the blog I thought, "I can't tell the truth. People won't read it." I was worried about what other people thought about me. I was worried that people would be able to see right through me. Everyone would know I was an insecure mess of a human who had no control over her life, and they would mock me.

It took me a while to find my voice and completely open up and be honest. What happened when I did that was truly amazing. People were reaching out to me and telling me that they felt the exact same way I did. One of my favorite things to do is read my email and messages on my social media accounts. They are filled with stories from people telling me that they can relate to me. They are writing to me to thank me for saying what they are feeling, and thanking me for being honest. They are telling me that they felt alone and insecure in their lives as well, and that my words brought them comfort. Finding my community, my tribe has been the most rewarding part of this entire journey. They make ignoring the haters easier. Making a connection with fellow parents and women who know what I am going through has been amazing and empowering.

"I can't poop" is part of a self-fulfilling prophecy. If we say that we can't, we won't. It's pretty simple. When our children say that they can't, we correct them and explain that we have to try and if we fail, we get up and try again. Why is it that as we get older we forget that lesson? My guess is that as the poop piles up and things become overwhelming, we state that we can't because our will to continue has been damaged or we have allowed the haters to win. If we say we can't when we fail, we make ourselves feel better by saying, "See, I knew I couldn't do it." When in fact what we actually did, was set ourselves up for failure. If we take the words "I can't" out of the equation, it will open up a world of possibilities. We need to be open to the idea that we can, in fact, be successful. We can conquer! We can achieve. We can, in fact, scoop the poop and continue on with our journeys.

I spent a majority of my time over the past two years worrying I was not going to succeed, worrying I was unable to reach or obtain my dream. This book is just one stop in the journey. This book is about knowing that I am not alone and that we all scoop the same poop, even if the haters continue to hate. Day in and day out, we live our lives in these social media charged, solitary islands, yet we think that everyone else is doing it right or doing it better. That simply isn't true. We are all met with very similar steamy piles of poop throughout our lives. We all scoop differently, but we must scoop none the less. There is no "I can't" while scooping the poop of life, or of parenting.

In terms of parenting, Mom shaming has gotten out of control. I have received many negative comments about my views on parenting and how I treat my children. Everyone seems to have an opinion on how someone else should parent. I am not sure why people feel it necessary to tell someone else that they are parenting wrong. I am all for people having and voicing opinions, but let's remember that opinions are not facts. It's like the whole breast vs bottle feeding issues that has gone crazy over the past year. Why on earth are people fighting over this? The only thing that matters is that you feed your child. I breast and bottle fed my children. Breast feeding was difficult for me and I know I was not the only woman who struggled with this. Why on earth should we shame a woman who is struggling? As parents we have very complicated jobs. We need to raise strong, independent humans who are hopefully not assholes. It is a freaking exhausting job. Save the shame and judgement, there is not a single parent on this planet who is doing it right all the time. That, I am a million percent sure of.

In the end, we need to use the hater poop to build ourselves up rather than to tear ourselves down. We are the only ones who can control our emotions. We can be whatever and whoever we want to be. Words cannot determine our worth and value. I had a frenemy once tell me that I hadn't been a success with my writing yet because I hadn't made any money. I replied, "My kids ate my earnings last night in the form of Hot Pockets, and they loved it." BOOM!

11. WHAT DOES ALL THIS POOP MEAN?

As we grow and change, our journey will take shape. At times we think we know what we want, but that can evolve in the blink of an eye. We can't give up on a dream because we are getting older. It is never too late. I woke up at thirty four years old and realized I could no longer put my dreams on hold. I decided that with three kids, a full time job, and a house to run, it was the perfect time to chase a dream.

It will never be easy. The shit storm that I have been involved in for over the past three years of my life has been all encompassing. At times it was too much. I wanted to quit. I tried to quit. But, I simply couldn't quit. I couldn't quit because there is so much to do and so many people to reach. I need parents to know that they are not alone in this journey. I need to make sure that everyone who needs this community can find it and take solace in knowing that they are not alone.

I am so excited for the future. I am so excited to head out into this big world and meet as many members of my tribe as I possibly can. I want to bring a message of hope and understanding that even after life's shit storms have ravaged us, there are rainbows: pretty, colorful, rainbows that shine down on our tired, broken asses, letting us know that it was all worth it.

We need to take some time to evaluate our secret poop. What is our massive turd hiding in the corner? What is it that we are keeping from everyone else? It is much easier to bring the poop into the light and tackle it head on. It was very difficult to tell my husband that I was unhappy and had a void in my life. I was terrified that he was going to be ashamed of me. I thought he was going to judge me for wanting more. I didn't think I was going to be able to figure out what I needed in my life, but guess what? I figured it out. It didn't happen overnight, but with thousands of hours of hard work, tears, laughter, fights, failures, and successes, I am still chasing the dream.

Many of us have health poop? Since starting this journey, I have had several women contact me to tell me that they are fighting breast cancer, ovarian cancer, and other major health battles. I was amazed and astonished by their will to fight and by their ability to find laughter along their heart wrenching journeys. I was completely humbled by their messages, where they thanked me for bringing them laughter and joy. To them, and everyone reading this, I thank you. I thank you for the support. I thank you for the friendship. I thank you for the community that has been created and developed so that many more can find this place and know that they have a home where we can support and encourage each other through life's toughest journeys.

Many of us dream, but get stuck in the "how" of getting started. I can attest that a little research can be helpful. When I decided that I wanted to write a blog, I went online and I looked at hundreds of various types of blogs. I had to figure out what I wanted to say, and I needed to find my voice. I spent hours reading posts and articles from other Mom bloggers, lifestyle bloggers, DIY bloggers, and entertainment bloggers. I knew that I wanted to make people laugh. I knew it wasn't going to be easy, but I had to work at finding my voice. No matter what goal we set, getting started is always the hardest part. It can be scary, and when we are unsure of ourselves it can be downright terrifying. There were plenty of times that I said to myself, "If I don't start writing, at least I won't fail." What I quickly realized is that, if I never started, I could never succeed.

As Moms, our Mom poop can be too much to scoop each day. The fighting, the mess, the drop offs and pick up, the homework; it can turn into a poop tornado. There is a reason they call it a grind, and I can tell you there are days I want to run away because I can't grind or scoop anymore. The times when I hide under my desk, or break down and cry in the McDonalds drive thru line are the times when the Mom poop is extra-heavy poop. When I know that the weight of the world which I have created falls directly on my shoulders, that poop is heavy, and at times can be crippling. That is why it is so important that we find time for ourselves and let go of the Mom guilt. Don't scoop poop that is unnecessary and self-destructive. Mom guilt can be debilitating. Let it go!

Who cares if the house is a mess, the laundry isn't done, and I haven't grocery shopped in two weeks. Guess what? It happens. My silverware drawer has mismatched spoons, forks, and knives. There are Taco Bell sauce packets and Captain Crunch crumbs in the cracks of the dividers. If anyone needs a used fast food straw, I've got those too. I have a kitchen table that is rarely maple syrup free, and I have come to terms with the fact that I no longer have nice things. If someone broke into my house, they would probably leave empty handed, unless they find value in broken VCR and DVD players, stained blankets, and broken furniture. We *live* in our home. The mess we live in once drove me crazy. I would clean up as the kids were playing. I would wipe every spill and wash every piece of laundry the same day it was soiled. The stress that the house poop caused me made me realize that it will never all get done. But, I can choose what to let go of. I can go to bed with dishes in the sink. I can wait to clean up the toy room until the kids go to bed, or better yet, I can leave it until the weekend. I have the power to scoop the house poop that I deem necessary. I choose to live in a home that looks lived in. If others can't handle that, they can scrub away. We all just need to know that we are the ones who set the priorities.

When we got married, I bet many of us weren't thinking, "I can't wait to scoop my lover's poop." We were thinking how amazing and wonderful our lives together would be. We were thinking about all of the incredible trips we would take, the children we would create, and the feeling we had at that moment in time in your heart. We were thinking about the passion, the connection we share with our spouses, but most likely, we were not thinking about the poop. Marriage is a relationship that we choose, but it is also a daily challenge. There are days when we are on a battle field with our mates, and days when we are so broken that we melt into each other's arms with no tears left to cry. No matter what happens in marriage, it is astonishingly important to scoop the poop so the relationship can remain strong. Marriage is a union by choice, we need to choose to prioritize our mates. We need to choose to scoop even when we are so tired we want to quit. We need to think back to why we chose them, and choose to scoop.

We all have dreams, even if we deny them. They are there. They are waiting to be fulfilled. They are important to us. Dreams are not an inconvenience. They are part of us. What do I want to be when I grow up? I use to laugh and tell my husband that I want to be him when I grow up. I decided that I don't have to choose. I can be everything I have worked for because growing up is a journey that I get to stay on until the day that I die. Adulting is difficult, and I choose to believe that I am still growing up. So I will scoop my dream poop so that I can continue to dream and chase to my heart's content. We should all continue to chase our dream poop.

We can pick our noses, we can pick our friends, but we can't pick our families. Family is an amazing gift, but it can also be an unbelievable pain in the ass. Our parents, our siblings, and our in-laws can cause us unbelievable amounts of stress and grief. We need to pick our battles. We can't scoop our families' poop for them. We need to let them own their poop and let them scoop it accordingly. We have plenty to scoop on our own, we do not need to own someone else's poop. It is difficult to tell family members no, but if we enable them, we will scoop their poop forever.

We all have personal poop. It took me a while to find out who I am. I am someone who rejects judgement. I am someone who chooses to laugh instead of cry. I am someone who has zero shits to give. If people don't like what I have to say, or how I choose to say it, they are welcome to read another book, watch another video, or find a different social media channel to patronize. I was once called a "liberal feminist who is single handedly tearing down traditional family roles by spreading lies." I had no idea I had the power to crush traditional families. I guess it is safe to say that I don't have a traditional family. It is also safe to say that I don't care . My family is *my* family. My poop is *my* poop.

If people don't have something nice to say, they shouldn't say anything at all. That old adage doesn't exist any longer. With social media, people can be torn apart on several platforms within a matter of minutes. Hater poop can be tough poop to scoop. Hater poop can cause emotional turmoil. Hater poop can cause people to doubt their self-worth. Try to remember that the hater being dealt with is in fact projecting their issues onto other people. Haters do not have control over us unless we give them the ability to do so. Hater poop can be extra smelly, but it is truly a reflection of the hater and not the target.

Think about what we could accomplish if we took the phrase, "I can't" out of our vocabularies. What if we had to put ourselves out there and be vulnerable? What if we took a minute out of each day and we told ourselves about the wonderful things that we accomplished that day. It doesn't need to be something major like running a marathon, it can be the simple things like "I folded the laundry AND I put it away in the same day". Wait, that is pretty major. But seriously, what if we gave ourselves the credit we deserve and we put ourselves out there enough to believe that we can accomplish our goals and fulfill our dreams. What if we first think, "I can" instead of automatically thinking, "I can't". It would be amazing to see the things that we would accomplish.

You are not alone. Your poop is no different than my poop. We all have to scoop the poop each day to make it through. Finding a poop scooping buddy can be very helpful in your journey. I think that community and friendships are imperative in scooping the poop. As humans we need to know that others can understand where we are coming from. We need to be heard. We need to be acknowledged. We need to feel validated. I wrote this book to unify a community. I wrote this book to bring people together. I wrote this book to let everyone know that we are not isolated islands. We are all going through the same things. We all have daily struggles. We all have meltdowns. We all have fights. We all have kids who push the limits. We all have bosses that drive us crazy. We all have families that over step boundaries. WE ALL HAVE TO SCOOP THE POOP. The way I look at it, we can scoop alone, or we can find people who have compassion and the ability to laugh and make poop jokes while we scoop together. I choose to scoop with my poop scooping buddies. I hope you will join me and be a part of the #Scoopthepoop movement.

ABOUT MEREDITH

I am a Mom. I had babies, not a lobotomy. I am here to tell stories about my life, my family, my struggles, and my joy. I try to find the humor in all things. I am on a quest to obtain my dreams. I want to become the best version of me. I want to be happy in both my professional and personal life. I want to share my voice, my stories, my humor, my tale.

I write about raw real life. I believe that real life is dirty and exhausting but we find joy despite the monotony of the daily grind.

I have been working towards creating a community of "Real Moms" who talk about the good, the bad, and the ugly side of parenting. I hope you will all join me in the #Scoopthepoop movement.

CPSIA information can be obtained
at www.ICGtesting.com
Printed in the USA
LVOW01s2314310117
522808LV00006B/158/P